Mstislav Rostropovich
and
Galina Vishnevskaya

Mstislav Rostropovich
and
Galina Vishnevskaya

Russia, Music, and Liberty

CONVERSATIONS WITH
CLAUDE SAMUEL

TRANSLATED BY
E. Thomas Glasow

AMADEUS PRESS
Reinhard G. Pauly, General Editor
Portland, Oregon

From the 1983 French-language edition:

Entretiens avec Mstislav Rostropovitch et Galina Vichnevskaïa could not have been written without the technical assistance of Nina Apreleff who, in the course of recording these interviews, faithfully translated questions and answers. Her perfect knowledge of the Russian language, her proven technique in the area of simultaneous interpreting, and her friendly ties with Galina Vishnevskaya and Rostropovich enabled her to preserve the liveliness, precision, and suggestive power of the dialogues.

Copyright © 1983 as
*Entretiens avec Mstislav Rostropovitch
et Galina Vichnevskaïa*
by Editions Robert Laffont, S.A., Paris.
Translation copyright © 1995 by Amadeus Press
(an imprint of Timber Press, Inc.)
All rights reserved.

ISBN 0-931340-76-4

Printed in Singapore

AMADEUS PRESS
The Haseltine Building
133 S.W. Second Avenue, Suite 450
Portland, Oregon 97204-3527, U.S.A.

Library of Congress Cataloging-in-Publication Data

Rostropovich, Mstislav, 1927–
    [Entretiens avec Mstislav Rostropovitch et Galina Vichnevskaïa. English]
    Mstislav Rostropovich and Galina Vishnevskaya : Russia, music, and
liberty / conversations with Claude Samuel ; translated by E. Thomas Glasow.
        p.   cm.
    Discography: p.
    Includes index.
    ISBN 0-931340-76-4
        1. Rostropovich, Mstislav, 1927–   . 2. Vishnevskaya, Galina, 1926–
3. Violoncellists—Interviews. 4. Sopranos (Singers)—Interviews.
I. Vishnevskaya, Galina, 1926–   . II. Samuel, Claude. III. Title.
ML418.R77A5 1995
780'.92'2—dc20   94-11669
        [B]   CIP
                                                                           MN

Contents

Preface

Sunday, 11 February 1990. The Sheremetyevo Airport is crawling with people. Men and women are asked to comment before the watchful eye of American television cameras. Not long before, only a handful of the curious had gathered; now there's a constant stream of newcomers. An extraordinary crush of humanity fills a private lounge, access to which was at first under tight control, now literally taken by storm.

At one end, the door opens to admit an arrival: Jack Lang, the French minister of culture. The waiting resumes. Impatience mounts. People hang on to something to avoid being pushed back. Suddenly, there's a rush for the door as it opens to admit more passengers. One can make out, even at twenty paces, the two wonders now revealed: Galina Vishnevskaya, her dignified smile hiding her emotion, Mstislav Rostropovich ready to distribute a thousand kisses among old friends. The crowd surges forward, lit by an incredible explosion of flashbulbs from the press corps. Slava calls out to faces overwhelmed with joy. Moments later, the two slip into a car and head for the Novodevichi Cemetery, where they will pay their respects at the graves of Prokofiev, Shostakovich, and David Oistrakh. They'll spend the night at the U.S. embassy.

The impossible dream had come true. What Galina couldn't imagine during the long years of exile ("And that day will not occur in my lifetime"), the phantom image that had haunted Slava's nights, was a reality. The regime that had seemed utterly impervious to change had, in the space of three or four years, begun to fall apart without war or revolutionary violence. Sixteen years after leaving the repression of the Soviet Union, Slava and Galina were back in a Russia suddenly reborn, a land where state police no longer harassed the nonconformist artist.

During those sixteen years, they had lived, thought, suffered, and hoped along with the pulse of events in "their" homeland, along with "their" people. Rostropovich publicly expressed his indignation over Brezhnev's tyranny and welcomed with great hope—tinged with skepticism—the change in political climate under Mikhail Gorbachev: "I subscribe to numerous Soviet newspapers, which I read day and night. What's happening is extremely interesting. Extraordinary things are taking place. I applaud the change, and would gladly take part in it. . . . Under Brezhnev, 200 million sheep would repeat in unison whatever he said. To tell them now that they were stupid—not even Gorbachev can do that. If he did, they'd respond: 'And what were *you*?' "*

Rostropovich had met Gorbachev some two years before, in late 1987, a year in which he played and conducted more

*Interview by Jacques Drillon in *Le Nouvel Observateur*, 9–15 September 1988, 43.

than ever, worldwide, in celebration of his sixtieth birthday, including a series of eighteen concerts in New York City. At Ronald Reagan's invitation, he and others came to the White House on 8 December to hear Van Cliburn perform in the presence of the new leader of Russia. The two exchanged a few words that night; no doubt Rostropovich thanked Gorbachev for having "freed" his sister Veronika earlier that year.

"I'm going to tell you a story about my sister. She is a violinist in Moscow. For ten years she dreamed of paying me a visit, but she was never granted a visa. Even when she was on tour with her orchestra, she couldn't leave. Then, just before President Reagan went to Reykjavik to meet Gorbachev, I asked him to put in a word for her. And she arrived. Just like that."*

Life goes on. The dazzling career of the world's most famous musician had continued. Weeks were spent on the podium before the National Symphony Orchestra, in Washington or on long international tours, a whirlwind punctuated by premieres of new works written for him by his composer friends Henri Dutilleux, Witold Lutoslawski, Cristóbal Halffter, Krzysztof Penderecki, Alfred Schnittke, and Sofia Gubaidulina.

In 1986, Galina, her singing career now divided between recitals and master classes, staged Rimsky-Korsakov's *The Tsar's Bride* at the Opéra de Monte-Carlo; Rostropovich conducted. A few months later, in Paris, he became the driving force behind the largest Prokofiev cycle ever organized in the world. One way to teach the Soviets a lesson! At first, his project was simply to conduct and record in concert the complete *War and Peace*. "Simply" is hardly the word: Prokofiev's work, inspired by Tolstoy's panoramic

---

*Interview by Isabelle Garnier in *Le Figaro Magazine*, 21 March 1987.

novel, calls for large orchestra and chorus, comprises sixty-three roles, and is over four hours long! Rostropovich entrusted me with this bundle of cares, and I must say, it took much conviction and stubborn determination to amass the necessary finances.

But for Slava (once again demonstrating the unselfish generosity which some spiteful souls wrongfully hold against him) it was a matter of sacred duty: Prokofiev, who had endured the mutilations the Stalin regime imposed on his opera, often said to his young friend, "I'd like to attend a complete performance of *War and Peace* before I die." Fate decreed otherwise, and thirty-three years after Prokofiev's death—on Sunday, 7 December 1986, to be precise—Rostropovich was back in the Salle Pleyel, conducting the Orchestre National de France and the Choeurs de Radio France in the long-awaited resurrection. Galina, in resplendent vocal form, sang the role of Natasha. Rostropovich spoke of the event: "I think the greatest thing I have done in my life is to have restored the opera *War and Peace* to its original form by scrupulously respecting Prokofiev's intentions. Curiously it parallels what is happening right now in Russia: people are beginning to scrape away the decades of bureaucratic filth that has accumulated around them."* Sixteen other concerts dedicated to Prokofiev made up the cycle. An act of defiance!

Three years later, once again in the capacity of opera conductor, Slava was less pleased. I imagine he would prefer to forget altogether the *Boris Godunov* (original 1869 version) that he led for a film soundtrack. The movie, offered to Tarkovsky a few weeks before that director's death, and then to Wajda, was ultimately left in the hands of Polish director André Zulawski. Sacrilegious hands, according to Slava once he'd seen the result. The provocative images coupled with the overmixing of Mussorgsky's score with various sound

---

*Interview by Jacques Doucelin in *Le Figaro*, 25 October 1988, 41.

effects (heavy breathing in the love scenes, the sound of the Fool urinating into a pail) were intolerable to both Rostropovich and Galina, who performs the role of Marina on the soundtrack. They demanded changes that the director refused to incorporate. It went to court, and—though it stopped short of eliminating the offensive material—the judgment required that a written notice clearly indicating the sentiments of the Rostropoviches be projected on screen at the beginning of the film.

In addition to his genuine indignation, which I could plainly see during a stormy private screening organized by the film's producer, Slava had the feeling that his imminent return to Moscow should not be clouded by a breach of taste against his Russian cultural heritage, that he would be reproached for having had a part in it. The case went to trial on 6 December 1989, and the verdict was decided the following 10 January, just one month before the disembarkation at Sheremetyevo Airport—an event which truly eclipses all else.

How to describe the reunions—first with friends, then two days later with the public! To microphones extended to catch first impressions, Slava explains, "I haven't seen anything yet. Only hugs and kisses, hugs and kisses!" On Monday, an emotional press conference, in particular, a call for justice for Solzhenitsyn. Tuesday, the first concert by the National Symphony Orchestra, with morning rehearsal open to the public. It's a struggle to get inside Conservatory Hall, and endless stamping of feet greets the hero's return. Slava raises his baton and begins the first notes of the Tchaikovsky "Pathétique"—the very symphony he had conducted just before his departure sixteen years before. Next, Samuel Barber's *Adagio for Strings* and Shostakovich's Fifth—the point of no return in the self-policing practiced under the Stalin era. Four encores, including a magisterial "Stars and Stripes Forever," bring to a glorious close an evening graced by the presence of Raissa Gorbachev and the queen of Spain, among other government officials and foreign ambassadors. Next the National Symphony went on to its second and final stop, Leningrad.

Had Rostropovich and Galina once more become "Soviet citizens"? Indeed, a few days prior to undertaking this first pilgrimage, they learned that the Supreme Soviet had decided to give them back their passports and medals. But Rostropovich—who, when the doors were only beginning to open, had declared, "We have committed no crime, so there's no question of our returning with heads bowed!"*— remained cautious. As he said during the heady days of January 1990, "I have confidence in Gorbachev but not yet in the Communists." †

In November of that same year, when he decided, on the spur of the moment, to perform before the symbolism of what remained of the Berlin Wall, by then thoroughly broken down, picked over, and trampled upon, Slava once more declared: "One must support Gorbachev, who has undertaken to change the mentality and the structure of his country. It won't be easy, for the U.S.S.R. has eighteen million ignorant bureaucrats earning enormous salaries who, in order to preserve their privileges, hope that nothing will change. And so mediocrity keeps its place." ‡

Rostropovich was right, and it wasn't long before the "mediocrity" of the entrenched manifested itself. The August 1991 uprising was a memorable moment in the history of international politics as well as in the life of Slava, who received the news on an ordinary day in his Paris apartment. "Of all the great occasions in my life, it is music that has guided the decisions I have had to make. On 19 August, when I learned of the revolt in Moscow, the music of Prokofiev, Shostakovich, Mussorgsky, and Stravinsky ran through my head, and I thought, with tears in my eyes, 'Here

*Interview by Jacques Doucelin in Le Figaro, 25 October 1988, 41.

†Paris Match, January 1990.

‡Le Figaro, 13 November 1990.

is a country that has given such geniuses to the world and yet continues to suffer.' I was immediately and irresistibly moved to leave for Moscow, secretly, without even taking time to carry my visa. A few hours later, I was in Moscow. . . . I passed entire hours at Boris Yeltsin's side. He conducted himself in an extraordinary manner. In seventy-four years, the first political figure to be elected by the [Russian] people!"*

Slava still has confidence in Boris Yeltsin: "He's the only one I believe in 100 percent." From Yeltsin he received the medal of "Defender of Free Russia." And it was again for "Free Russia" that he led his Washington musicians in Tchaikovsky's *1812 Overture*, in September 1993 in Red Square, while Yeltsin took on a Parliament bent on revenge!

The rest belongs to the future. We know that in 1994 Rostropovich will leave the post that has transformed the National Symphony Orchestra and given it unprecedented prestige. We know he will premiere a new opera by Shchedrin in Stockholm, and a new opera by Schnittke in Vienna. We know that October 1994 will find him in Paris, for the fifth time chairing the jury of the cello competition that bears his name. Finally, we know that he will remain faithful to his friends, notably to those who called on him in 1977 to head the Aldeburgh Festival, and to those who have entrusted him with the directorship of the Festival d'Evian since 1987.

The release (on disc and video) of Bach's six monumental Suites for Unaccompanied Cello, which Slava recorded in the Basilique de Vézelay in March 1991, is eagerly anticipated—a reminder that this extraordinary man was first and foremost a brilliant cellist. He possesses that rarest of qualities in celebrated soloists: the gift of sharing. In June 1988, upon launching the first worldwide cello conference at

---

Mélomane, October 1991.

the University of Maryland, he declared, "I invite all my cellist colleagues to join me in this celebration of our beloved instrument. Our service, through the universal language of music, can bring the world closer to peace."

—Claude Samuel
Paris, 1993

Introduction

I knew them in the era of silence—silence and glory. Galina, queen of the Bolshoi, came to Paris to show us the pathetic tenderness of Tatiana. From his seat in the royal box, the Soviet ambassador waved to the full house. When the applause finally subsided, Tatiana appeared. It would have been interesting to know what the queen of the Bolshoi was thinking at that moment.

As for Slava, he was already communicating. His bow danced, sang, rejoiced, flashed, as he made even the most trifling music stir our hearts. With all due respect to the great composers, he assumed the imposing tasks of teaching us the cello repertoire and performing the Don Quixotes of contemporary music. At a time when we Parisians swore by the innovative Domaine Musical, we would have liked him to concentrate on less reactionary stuff, but for those living under the reign of Khrennikov,* such distinctions no doubt meant very little.

One day, Slava told me he wanted to get to know the music of Olivier Messiaen. I sent over a recording of *Quatuor pour la fin du temps*, which—I'm told—he listened to all night long. I then urged Messiaen to write a work for cello, as soon as possible. The result wasn't quite the concerto that Slava had hoped for, but rather a concertante work in which he was only one of seven soloists. He played it soulfully, with all his heart, but with an obvious sense of frustration.

Another time I tried a bolder experiment: I had him listen to Xenakis's *Nomos alpha*, the shattering stridency of which had just electrified audiences at the Festival de Royan. At that time, every Soviet artist worthy of the name might as well have just arrived from the planet Mars. In fact, Slava's first question was something like, "What metal is the planet Mars made of?" Walking the Red Planet and Red Square were clearly two very different matters. Yet, later on, he played *Nomos alpha* as he promised me he would.

Slava and Galina immediately became part of our musical family. Their concerts and recitals spiced up our Parisian seasons, and the post-concert receptions gave us a chance to mingle with our new friends from the East. While Galina was always reserved and enigmatically pleasant, Slava was liberal with his embraces. Nevertheless, recalling a confidential remark that had slipped out inadvertently three years before, they would disappear as soon as their exit visas expired. One could then only imagine what they might be doing, in their gilded cage of a *dacha*. French composers sometimes returned the favor, in the shadow of the Kremlin.

No one ever actually spoke of the Kremlin, however. Galina remained inscrutable behind her winning smile. Slava would come up with phrases in a wild Anglo-Franco-Germanic pastiche before summoning help from the blond

*Tikhon Khrennikov, Soviet composer born in 1913. Deputy to the Supreme Soviet and first secretary of the Composers' Union of the U.S.S.R.

Nina, his indispensable interpreter, who would explain everything—except the long process by which one of the most renowned Soviet musicians became aware of the forced lies, everyday hypocrisy, and bogus freedoms.

Galina had cautioned her husband to be careful: the veil of oppression is not raised with impunity. Nevertheless, a latent rebel convinced that his art would protect him, Slava embarked on a path of denunciation. Protest led to repression, which drove them both to revolt. The Iron Curtain parted for the angry fugitives and their two daughters. Their Parisian friends greeted them with open arms, but had they considered the consequences of uprooting? They understood when silence turned into protest—notably on that March morning in 1978 when, during the course of an impromptu press conference, the pair reacted to the revocation of their Soviet citizenship, which they had learned of only the day before from a television newscast. Galina was by turns a tigress, a saddened Tosca, a thunderstruck Leonore. A dumbfounded Slava appealed movingly to international morality: "This is an inhuman and illegal act which effectively deprives us of the right to live and die in our own land!"

"Our land" remains the leitmotif of their existence. Throughout the course of our conversations, it was "our people" and even "our government." Paris, Lausanne, London, New York, Washington—all are merely so many temporary stopovers where the family sets up household after household without establishing roots. Each city is more cosmopolitan than the last, and yet Russian icons keep sentinel in each dwelling. Who can describe all the nostalgia whispered by Slava in a given concerto andante, all the sadness of a melodic phrase caressed by Galina? Public statements give one account, but to those who can hear it, the subtle shading of a musical phrase reveals a deep-rooted sadness. Slava embraces the world in order to make the wait for his return to the Promised Land the more bearable. Impassable threshold! Galina, alone in her resignation, no longer even believes in the Promised Land. Daughters Olga and Elena are already conquering a new world. To forget? To hope.

That idealistic hope is not often expressed in words, linked as it is to dark events which no one here has any control over. Yet, deafening in its silence, it is the main thread of these conversations, recorded and transcribed over the course of some thirty months on the initiative of Charles Ronsac, who is always on the lookout for great human, artistic, and/or political documentaries. So many months to express truths already so matter-of-fact and obvious for those who know our interlocutors? Yes, for the hardest task was tracking down an international virtuoso and juggling his calendar, even for a half-hour appointment, and then making that rendezvous fit the demands of a diva who is happily pursuing a recital career. Little by little, between Paris and Washington, the dialogue came together. From the outset, it was clear that it would be musical in flavor. But who knows better than Galina or Slava that music is at the core of the sorrows and joys of our everyday lives?

From the subject of music, we turned to Russia, and from Russia, to the subject of freedom. The progression was inevitable, and whatever the question, we kept returning, relentlessly, to these same areas of discussion. This the reader will be able to tell, but what one cannot see on the page and should keep in mind is the tone of the interviews: vehement, ironic, impassioned. Two impetuous personalities shouting their truth is hardly chamber music, but the great roar of a symphony orchestra. How can one avoid raising one's voice when the testimony is so scathing?

Showered with Flowers

Claude Samuel: The personal life of a great artist is an inexhaustible subject, shifting between the anecdotal and the mythic. You two are no exception to that rule: the story of your lives weaves a tale of love at first sight and marriage immediately thereafter. Is this a fairy tale?

Galina Vishnevskaya: No. Everything written about it is exactly correct.

Mstislav Rostropovich: I hate to disappoint you but it's absolutely true. Even if I wanted to, I couldn't tell it any other way. Still, I've noticed that, as they grow older, people start embellishing their past. It was my mother's habit. I remember she used to love to tell me all kinds of stories. When she was nearly eighty, she would still use direct quotations in recalling events that went back half a century: "So, he asked me . . . ," "I thought for a moment and answered . . ." I knew

19

those stories by heart, but I am sure she made them up, pure and simple! Fifteen years from now, if we're still around, I imagine we'll be telling stories that are just as fascinating—

C.S. Let's jump ahead fifteen years!

G.V. Very well. In May of 1955 I was a member of the Bolshoi company, where I had been singing for four seasons. I was interpreting leading roles and well on my way to becoming a star. I knew some famous artists, artists already at the peak of their careers, but no young ones like Rostropovich. Rostropovich? I had never even heard him play! Then one fine day, I met him in a restaurant, during a governmental reception. We were introduced, and that was all for the moment. Two weeks later, we met up again in Prague. I was invited by the Prague Spring Festival to sing the role of Tatiana—always Tatiana! Slava was giving some concerts and was on the jury of an international cello competition. It was my first tour abroad; I was very impressed by the city of Prague, by the beauty and atmosphere of the old town, by the manners and distinction of the people.

M.R. We went for a walk in the park—

G.V. On the day I arrived, I glimpsed him in a restaurant. He decided on the spot I was for him, and he set to work arranging a series of surprises. So the next morning, when I got up and opened my closet door, I discovered my clothes had been completely covered with lilies. The following day I found orchids in all four corners of my room. Truly show-ered with flowers! The third day, the floor was strewn with boxes of chocolates. That was the day I was supposed to leave to return to Moscow. Slava had other engagements, but without hesitating, he canceled them and followed me. On the fourth day, we were married, united for life.

C.S. And all those flowers—

M.R. —made her burst out laughing—

G.V. No they didn't; it was all your stories that made me laugh!

M.R. She would laugh until there were tears in her eyes. She'd hold her head in her hands to keep wrinkles from developing!

C.S. Was music the explanation for the speed of your mutual attraction?

G.V. Music? He hadn't heard me sing and I hadn't heard him play. We heard each other for the first time six months after we got married.

M.R. But if we hadn't been musicians, our personalities would have been different. Art plays an enormous role in the formation of a human being. But since all this happened in Prague, I'd like to take this chance to talk about Czechoslovakia. I'm looking forward to the day when I can return, for many events in my life connect me with that country—sometimes painful events like, for example, my refusal to go back to Prague after the Soviet invasion, a refusal which did nothing to better my situation in Russia.

Vladimir Popov, the vice-minister of culture, summoned me to his office and announced, "David Oistrakh has just played in Prague, and now it's your turn to go because our relations with Czechoslovakia have to be strengthened." I replied that I could not accept that proposition; I explained that after Soviet tanks entered Prague, it was impossible for me to appear on a stage before an audience of Czechs.

My first foray abroad, in 1947, was to Czechoslovakia. The

first "First International Prize" I received was in Czechoslovakia. The first record I made abroad, in 1950, was also in Czechoslovakia: the Dvořák Concerto under the direction of Václav Talich. And, as if that weren't enough, we were married in Prague. I had decided to go back to Czechoslovakia every five years with Galina to celebrate the event; in 1960, after the first five years, we did indeed go back, and again in 1965, again in the month of May, but then it was no longer tolerable. People there were not able to hide their animosity toward the Soviet Union, or should I say their contempt!

G.V. Everywhere, in the restaurants, in the hotels, we encountered nothing but hostile looks.

M.R. So, since I had so many fond personal memories of Czechoslovakia, I decided to stop going there, to wait for the time when I can see the Czechoslovakians really free. When they are truly happy.

C.S. If you were invited to Prague today, would you refuse?

M.R. Yes, I want to see the people happy. I wouldn't want my presence, my Russian presence, to provoke their hatred of the system. Obviously Czech journalists, like their Soviet counterparts, cannot write anything, cannot publish the smallest protest against the regime. Their only possible means of expression is their outward physical comportment. I understand them very well, but it's very painful to me.

C.S. However, your current status could bring you closer together.

M.R. Of course. They themselves can change their attitude but, in any case, they no longer have the right to invite me. Which reminds me of the story of the hen and the barley seed. There was this man who thought he was a barley seed and who had been placed in a psychiatric clinic. Some time later, during a routine examination, he says to the doctor, "You know, I was sick. I thought I was a barley seed, but that's all over. I'm cured."

"Good. Go back home," the doctor replied. A half-hour later, the man comes running back, wild-eyed:

"You know what? On my way home, I saw a hen!"

"Yes," says the doctor, "but you *know* you're not a barley seed!"

"Sure, *I* know it, but does the *hen* know it?"

The same goes for my relations with the Czechoslovakians. *I* know I love them, but do *they* know?

C.S. Prague is the chapter of nostalgia and hope. Let's return to your meeting, which soon gave birth to a musical duo. An unexpected event—

G.V. Indeed, in those days, when I gave recitals, it was always Boris Abramovich who would accompany me. One day, some time after our wedding, when I was scheduled to sing in Tallinn with Abramovich, Slava suddenly told me:

"I am going to accompany you!"

"What are you saying? *You* are going to accompany me? Why, you're crazy, you don't know how to play the piano. I thought you were a cellist!"

"I swear, I can also play the piano. I played a Rachmaninoff concerto at the Conservatory."

"Yes, but I need an accompanist who is used to working with singers."

"I'll work at it every day, I promise you!"

M.R. That's true. Galina didn't have any confidence in my capacity as a pianist. But I wanted to spend as much time as possible with her, so I decided to return to the piano. I had obviously lost the basics of my pianistic ability because I wasn't able to devote all my time to that instrument. And today I take delight in thinking that some day my accompanying Galina will surprise people. That will be the day I begin working three weeks before a concert, since I usually start studying a new piece three days before the concert. And when that time comes, no one will recognize me!

G.V. You frighten me! Better that you not practice and continue to play the way you do now!

M.R. In any case, it was for Galina that I went back to the piano, and my happiness is being at her side during her recitals. But her other accompanists sometimes jealously objected. We had a few serious scenes, true scandals!

You know, outwardly, people often completely misjudge what occurs between a couple. For this reason I no longer give the least bit of credence to rumors that circulate about other couples. At any rate, I recall, for example, the difficulties I encountered with Galina's usual pianist. Why couldn't he accept the fact I wanted to play with her simply in order to spend the maximum amount of time in her company? I wanted to participate in Galina's artistic performances, I wanted to "accompany" her. I think that's a beautiful word,"accompany." There are people who think it has a negative connotation; not I. I was happy to accompany Galina. But her pianist made a fuss in front of me and cried, "Do you really need the money? Isn't your career making enough headway?" I was obliged to explain at great length to him that I was making very little money as an accompanist, for I had no qualification as a pianist. I mean, no official qualification. In fact, the rates of remuneration are calculated according to a precise scale in a State register, and the qualification also gives one access to different classes of railroad travel. In the Soviet Union, there are three classes: "international" uses a kind of international car, though without going abroad; second class, called "soft cars" since they have cushions, and third class, "hard cars" which have only wooden seats. As a cellist, I had the right to a soft car but as a pianist, to a hard car. When I would travel with Galina, I was always terribly hurt because Galina would be given a seat in a soft car and I was given a ticket for the hard car. So I'd telephone the administration and say, "I'll pay the difference if you give me a seat in the same class as Galina."

It was really in order to get closer to Galina and her art that I began to accompany her. Who would ever believe that the one person who fought with me, who tried to prevent me from going to the Bolshoi, was none other than Galina! And when she protested she'd break into tears, as is proper for a woman of temperament!

G.V. No, no one ever believed it. Everybody was convinced that it was I who had brought Slava to the theater, that I had dragged him there—

C.S. And why did you want to prevent him from coming to the Bolshoi?

G.V. Because I had *my* place at the Bolshoi and didn't want him to get mixed up in my professional life. I already knew what he was like and knew that, once he arrived at the theater, he would immediately get to know all the personnel, from the greatest star to the humblest ticket-taker, that he was going to hug and kiss everyone, that he'd invite the stagehands and the technicians and who knows who else for a drink and dinner with him, and that everybody would ultimately end up in my home, at the house. To this day, all the waitresses at the Bolshoi commissary lament his absence, because he'd gather up the busboys, the waitresses, all the regular staff, he'd gather everyone up and offer them a round of drinks. It was very nice, but the downside was that all the gossip of the Bolshoi started to drift toward my home. It was to keep that from happening that I didn't want him to come—

25

C.S. And then he came—

G.V. Obviously, he came! Everything happened just as I had feared.

M.R. And when I conducted my first production at the Bolshoi, I must say that Galina was not particularly nice to me. That first production was *Eugene Onegin*.

C.S. But weren't you nevertheless happy to be working together in the same theater?

G.V. No!

M.R. She wasn't happy because she was jealous of that place where she was building her career. She would say to me, "You work in the Conservatory and do whatever you want there. The Bolshoi is *my* house, it's *my* life. Don't stick your nose in there or you'll spoil everything for me! You can choose any theater, but not that one!" I was terribly annoyed. But even so, I came to the Bolshoi. I won! Galina must understand that she too won: when we went on tour together, for example when I conducted *Tosca* at Vilnius, she was traveling, in fact, with "her" conductor. I knew how she sang, and after the performance, I was always the willing scapegoat.

C.S. When you perform together in public, isn't there a special rapport between you? For example, does Galina sing as she would under another conductor?

M.R. No, she sings differently when I conduct. I can assure you, she takes liberties that she would never risk with another conductor!

G.V. It's to be expected. Since he always wants to do the opposite of what I do, well, I do the opposite of what I would have done without him. But that works only with opera. During concerts, there is no dissension between us. But, at the opera!

C.S. The public is naturally unaware of these subtleties, but it isn't unaware of the fact that you are married—

G.V. *We* know!

M.R. And we never think about it.

C.S. You are specialists in family music-making. A few years ago, for the twenty-fifth anniversary of your meeting, you even gave a concert in Paris with your two daughters, Elena the pianist and Olga the cellist. Could either of them have gone into anything other than music?

G.V. I considered it natural for them to study music. They studied for ten years at the Central School of Music, a respected establishment attached to the Moscow Conservatory. They had to become true professionals. If they had settled for taking private lessons, they wouldn't have devoted enough time to them; they would have had other desires and pastimes. In this school, there were several hours of music per day. No time to go out and play!

M.R. I would add that they began by taking dance. Olga sang and danced; she was driven by the boundless enthusiasm of her public! But it was first necessary for her to study piano, and she herself said to me at the age of twelve, "I want to play the cello." At school, she always received the best grades for her written work, so if she had decided to become a writer, I wouldn't have objected at all. But she chose music, the cello, and I approved.

G.V. Not long ago in Hong Kong, I attended a recital Slava

gave with Elena. You can imagine the happiness of a mother on such an occasion, and it wasn't even the first time I had heard them play together. I had already heard them at the White House, in the Salle Gaveau in Paris, in London, in Japan, in Scandinavia, in Argentina. Their duo is a veritable dialogue in which, as Slava said after their most recent concert, each partner is equal.

As for Olga, it's true that she freely chose the cello and is pursuing a career as a soloist. But she is cautious, like her father. Furthermore, she is gifted in very different fields and endlessly searches for new outlets for her energy and talent. Recently, Slava and I were surprised to discover she was modeling for Lanvin. Slava made a special trip to the United States to see her in that new role. I don't think I've ever seen him clap so hard. "You see," he said to me, "it's our beloved that the public is applauding!" Slava told me that the next day, when he got on the Concorde, the stewardess gave him a copy of *France-Soir*. His jaw dropped. There, on the front page, was a magnificent photo of his daughter. He jumped for joy, went from champagne to vodka, and circulated among the passengers, telling them, "You know, that's my daughter!"

Olga doesn't have the desire to be a professional model. The cello is her career. But so many things interest her. Who knows, maybe tomorrow she'll write a book or start painting.

We are so happy to see that our daughters are free, that with total liberty they choose their way of life and the country in which they'll live. They are following paths they have set for themselves and are spared the painful setbacks that we knew in the Soviet Union.

M.R. For some time now, in the morning when I shave, I look at myself in the mirror. And I say to Elena and her husband Peter, "I believe I'm physically ready to become a grandfather— Think about it!"

Talents and Talk

C.S. What is music? A job, a vocation, a passion?

G.V. For me, music is life. I couldn't have lived without it and cannot even imagine that possibility. Without music, I think I'd die!

M.R. She most certainly would have lived, and she would have worked, like everybody. But if she were not a singer, Galina would be another woman entirely, and I wouldn't even recognize her on the street—   Everything would have been different: she wouldn't have green eyes and her figure wouldn't be the same. Her figure? Yes, when Madame tries to slim down, *I'm* the one who suffers, *I'm* the one prevented from eating. I have to keep from eating so as not to stimulate her appetite, for she has only to gain one pound for life to become completely impossible!

Her life is so conditioned by art, and art illuminates her

face and spirit to such an extent, that her eyes would have been another color if she didn't sing. Her beauty would have been different.

G.V. I've always wanted to be on the stage and always knew that I had to perform. When I began to sing, I was very young and had a naturally placed voice. Since my mother was Tzigane [a Hungarian gypsy], I used to sing the folk songs that she had taught me. Even as a little girl, I adored performing in public. When friends would come to the house, I didn't have to be coaxed; I sang quite willingly and with all the more pleasure when there were listeners around. Therein lies, in fact, the primary quality of an artist, whereby one judges the genuineness of his or her vocation: the desire to practice one's art not for oneself but for others. Genuine artists feel the need to communicate their art.

M.R. I don't agree with Galina. At any rate, it's not my character, and Galina really must admit that I'm telling the truth. My character? It was Shostakovich who once said, "Rostropovich is truly gifted for everything." If I were to present you with a list of all the things I've done in life, the alternatives would be obvious— When I was a student, I earned a little money by framing paintings. Later on, totally by chance and because there was no one else to do it, I built a coffin, and to thank me, my professor gave me a bottle of cognac. I should say that we were then in the countryside and that a servant had just died. Now, in springtime, all roads being impassable, the body couldn't be transported to Moscow, nor could a coffin be delivered. There *was* an electric commuter train that served the suburbs, but putting a coffin on it was out of the question. I remember the days when, if it was impossible to bury a body due to impassable roads, people would dress it, put a hat on its head, slip a coat on it, and take it on the commuter train, as though it were someone who had fainted— To return to my story, we had to arrange a way to move it, and in that little village where there were more educated people than manual laborers, I was the one who had to figure out a way. Anyhow, I made an excellent coffin, though so heavy it was impossible to lift it. So I built only the frame, and to make it lighter, used plywood for the cover!

Whenever something broke in the house, I was the one who repaired it, even a sewing machine. Maybe I couldn't have repaired a watch as sophisticated as the one I'm wearing on my wrist, but large clocks—yes, I could fix them. I did all the electrical wiring for our house in Moscow— I don't think there's a profession I couldn't have taken up.

C.S. A doctor, for example?

M.R. Oh yes, certainly! I would have liked to be a doctor, and I could also have been a lawyer, to help people— But, as a child, I dreamt of very simple jobs: I wanted to be a chauffeur or to build houses, not as an architect but as a mason, for I really needed to get my hands on bricks and mortar and to work on the construction site.

Music then would have played a part in my life, but it would have existed only for me. Galina, you say you have to give music to others, but I felt that my own emotions were fulfilling enough. I recall that at seven or eight years old I had tears in my eyes while listening to the *Symphonie pathétique*. My parents were delighted. Then, instead of soothing me, they would continue to supply me with my dose of music. At the time, I felt music so intensely that I was content to live in solitude.

The first time I had the joy of communicating music to others, I was fifteen and taking part in a series of theme programs. There was an "evening of waltzes and serenades," for instance. It was also a way to earn a little money. To be paid, you had to play three pieces. I had no problem selecting the first two, for they were always ready in my repertoire: Tchaikovsky's *Valse sentimentale* and Glazunov's *Sérénade espagnole*. But I had to practice the third one at the last minute. That's how I learned a waltz by Kreisler entitled *Liebesleid* [Love's Sorrow]. When I appeared onstage in the short pants of a youth and the dull announcer intoned, "Slava is now going to play for you *Liebesleid*," the audience burst out laughing and I wasn't able to begin my piece.

That's when I became aware of what an audience is, of what they like or don't like. And that's when my personal feeling about music changed. I began to understand that you had to play for others.

G.V. So, I was right!

M.R. No. You said that you wanted to sing for others from the start. With me, the feeling manifested itself later.

G.V. The day you became an artist! That's precisely the difference between a professional artist and an amateur artist. The amateur performs for his own pleasure, while the artist is drawn to the stage and wants to address the public. This desire to play for others can be called the vocation.

M.R. Yes, it can be called the vocation. But, as far as Galina is concerned, I would add that she is a naturally great actress. Since her childhood she has been attracted by the stage and sought contact with the public.

G.V. And you want us to believe that you play your best only in the privacy of your own room?

C.S. Slava, wouldn't you have liked being an actor—

M.R. I would have adored being an actor, but I knew it was impossible since I had a speech impediment and, moreover, I knew my "type" for what it was. I would have been turned down for romantic leads and forced to play nothing but comic roles— I must say my parents didn't endow me with a great physique!

C.S. Galina, do you think Slava would have been a good actor?

G.V. I'm not sure, not sure at all. One can be very brilliant and witty in life, but to go on the stage one must possess other qualities. In the theater, everything happens as if the temperature were a few degrees warmer. If in real life my temperature is 98.6, onstage I register at least 200!

M.R. At 200 degrees, you would be playing your role in heaven!

G.V. Now wait, you must understand what I'm saying! What I don't like about the theater today is that actors force themselves to behave onstage as they do in real life. They stop practicing their diction and speak with simple, ordinary voices. This is why the great tragedies are so difficult to produce these days; they require well-placed voices and a completely different way of handling the body. But now, actors step onto the stage without any preparation, and curiously, it seems that the public takes a certain pleasure in seeing people who resemble them. Hire a singer without a voice and half the public will enjoy attending the performance, thinking they could do just as well!

When I make *my* entrance on the stage, I want to achieve what the majority of people are incapable of achieving, and I try to give my all. Whether the theater is large or small, whether it's the Paris Opéra or a pocket-size theater, is not important. On that day, I summon up all my concentration to meet that demand. I must also be physically at my best; even my hair has to be just right! When I am onstage, I cannot permit myself the least oversight or the slightest imperfection. On days when I am to go onstage, my whole life is different; from the moment I get out of bed in the morning, everything is different.

M.R. I think Galina is right. I wouldn't have been a good actor. I've just thought about it, and I believe that performing the role of someone else, not being myself, would have been extremely boring for me.

G.V. You are incapable of dissembling. You are as natural in music as you are in social relations, while in the theater, one must playact, one must imitate.

C.S. Isn't interpreting a musical composition, in a certain way, like getting into a role?

M.R. No, it's another thing altogether. It's my own spirit that is invested in the music. There is no transformation, either in my body or my personality. I communicate my interpretation and remain myself. It would be rather comical if I were to play a work of Prokofiev as though he himself were at the piano! That's the fundamental difference between an actor and a musical interpreter.

G.V. Music and theater belong to two different worlds. In music, one cannot change the slightest note; all the material is strictly imposed, given to the performer. In theater, one isn't tied in the same way to a mandatory passage of time; the text is written down, but the manner of communicating it may vary, and even if the actor changes a word, it isn't catastrophic—whereas in opera, nothing can be moved around. The performer is given all the musical elements and must insert his own personality into them. Even in a ballet, a dancer may change a step and the audience won't notice it—

C.S. You perhaps underestimate the knowledge of ballet audiences—

G.V. Of course, certain specialists will notice, but they are greatly in the minority. In singing, however, the high note is right there on paper; you cannot sing another one!

C.S. Slava, what happens when you conduct an opera? When you're in the pit, do you forget you're in the theater?

M.R. Oh, no! Not at all! I like to live, suffer, feel with the singers. I'm not onstage, but I am at their side; I live and suffer right along with them. A poet like Pushkin, when he was writing *Eugene Onegin,* lived with his characters and suffered along with them. That's exactly how I feel when I conduct an opera.

For example, I recall the time I was in Moscow with a great many worries; I had to go to the offices of the Goskonzert to overcome innumerable difficulties, I had colleagues at the Conservatory who were displeased about I don't know what— But the minute I arrived at the Bolshoi, and the curtain rose to reveal the Larin country estate, I thought to myself, "How happy I am to be among them, to share their life."

While on this subject, I'd like to tell a very interesting anecdote concerning a performance of *Eugene Onegin* in Moscow. As you know, the overture begins with pizzicatos in the double basses. Now, before I could give the double basses their cue, even before arriving at the rehearsal, I wanted to smell the scent of hay and to show how the pizzicato had to be attacked gently, with vibrato. I had already entered into the atmosphere of *Onegin*. Well, that particular day, I look up and see the Soviet hammer and sickle on the great Bolshoi curtain. I went backstage and said that I could not conduct in front of a curtain that removed me so far from the world of

Eugene Onegin. And, sure enough, I got them to put up a white curtain for the production of *Eugene Onegin.*

C.S. I've always been struck by your uncanny ability to visualize music. During a rehearsal, you don't say, "Play *fortissimo!*" but instead, "Play as if you were slamming a door!"

M.R. Indeed, music evokes images and thought associations in me.

C.S. Whereas your compatriot Igor Stravinsky claims that music expresses nothing—

M.R. I don't believe it, and he didn't believe it himself. I knew his feelings, his love for Tchaikovsky—and, in any case, Tchaikovsky's music always has an emotional content. Music is not only an arrangement of sounds. Obviously, everyone can interpret it as he wishes, but for my part, I cannot accept that statement by Stravinsky.

C.S. Have you always had, shall we say, a "romantic" conception of music? Yet the word "romantic" makes you uncomfortable—

M.R. No, not at all, on the contrary! I think that art and life are totally intertwined. When I was young, I would fall in love easily and not expect to be loved in return; so, I suffered, which brought out chivalrous sentiments in me. I always had the desire to rescue someone. I could make sacrifices in order to make a friend happy. I was capable of staying up all night to be the life of the party if I were asked to.

C.S. Galina, is Slava cut out for suffering?

G.V. Yes, I believe he needs it. Any great artist must have a tendency toward suffering. Yet, contrary to what one might think, it doesn't destroy you—quite the opposite, it forces you to gather up your strength to dominate it, and at that moment, you get a better grip on the situation at hand.

C.S. Which for a musician implies technical mastery. How were you able to acquire it, Slava, in the beginning?

M.R. It was all easy, always easy, because it's a question of muscle and hand coordination, and those were qualities my parents handed down to me. Thus, I never practice at my piano, and I can stop playing the cello for a month at a time. When I return to my instrument, my fingers hurt—but I need only work at it for a day; the following day, no traces of my hiatus remain.

C.S. Who decided you would be a cellist?

M.R. There was no "decision"; everything happened naturally. My father was a cellist, and my first memories—the memories that remain embedded in a four-year-old's mind— are of my father playing the cello. But if he had played badly, I don't think I ever would have wanted to play myself.

C.S. What sort of a career did he have?

M.R. He was an absolutely phenomenal cellist. He was also an excellent pianist. He played everything by heart. And he was an extraordinary sight-reader; I must say that I never met another performer as gifted in the art. He wanted to acquaint me with the piano repertoire, and I recall how he sight-read a Rachmaninoff concerto: it was miraculous! I don't say all the notes were right there, but it was on the whole absolutely extraordinary.

C.S. Did he have a career as a soloist?

M.R. No, he was a man who had no lucky breaks, and despite his gifts, he didn't have the drive necessary to pursue a career. A question of character—   I imagine it must have been hard on him. He used to say, "If they need me, they'll come and get me!" I'd add that there were extenuating circumstances, since my uncle, the husband of my mother's sister, who was also a cellist, would get all the good positions and land all the contracts. My father died a complete unknown.

C.S. He's the one who taught you the cello?

M.R. Yes, it was he. I was thin as a rail then; I barely had any strength, and the first time I played with an orchestra, I had a lot of trouble making myself heard. I suffered. That was during my adolescence.

C.S. But the first school, the first conservatory?

M.R. That was the Moscow School of Music.

C.S. And the teachers with whom you studied?

M.R. My father! That's all!

C.S. You didn't have any other teachers?

M.R. Yes. After my father's death, I did study with that uncle who ruined my father's chances for a career. My father had left a letter, found after his death, in which he explained I had to finish my studies with my uncle. But if it hadn't been for that letter, I never would have studied with that uncle!

C.S. And, of course, you had begun to compose?

M.R. Obviously. I wrote some piano concertos and also composed a romance, but almost nothing for the cello. There was a time when I played the piano very well, and yet everyone confused me by assuring me that I was destined not to be an instrumentalist but a composer. Shostakovich, who was my teacher at the Moscow Conservatory, phoned my mother: "Slava must give up the cello to take up composition." At the Conservatory, I even received the only scholarship that had been distributed that year to pupils in the composition class and which bore the name of Tchaikovsky. But, ultimately, I'm very happy I didn't follow the advice of Shostakovich. During the course of my studies, I went through more compositional phases, sometimes feeling a sudden desire to compose—and everything seemed to be going well. But, all of a sudden, I was up against a wall, unable to write a note.

Today, from time to time, I sit at the piano and improvise, but only when I'm alone. Nevertheless I would like to have written a score for a play—

C.S. Any regrets?

M.R. No, truly not! I don't feel deprived in the least.

C.S. It was while you were in school, the period when you were choosing your path in life, that you knew two famous composers: Prokofiev and Shostakovich.

M.R. It was actually because of them that I stopped composing. I was so devoted to them and admired them so much! I worshipped them! Prokofiev would sometimes entrust me with his scores in their piano version while asking me to transcribe them into their definitive form. He wrote down very precise indications in parentheses beforehand—the orchestral scoring, for example—and the whole thing went like clockwork. His method greatly amazed me, for it surely took him more time than if he had written down the definitive score himself.

C.S. Thus, the genius of Prokofiev involuntarily crushed your talent as a composer. Let's say, more seriously, that you had the chance to learn your profession as a musician in a particularly favorable environment. Which was not the case for Galina.

G.V. Ah, no! Not at all!

M.R. No. No external factor predisposed Galina to her career, nothing encouraged her except for that great desire to surpass oneself, to be number one, and to reject anything that smacked of inferiority. All her strengths still focus on that ambition. And her strengths are considerable. To give a precise example, I must say that no other woman I know is able to get herself ready to go out in public as rapidly as she. If she has overslept and has only three minutes to get herself together before catching a plane, she'll use those three minutes to put on her makeup, to fix her hair, to wash up obviously—and she will be ready on time. You won't see her until those three minutes are up, for she needs three minutes, but three minutes suffice for her. Whatever the situation that confronts her, Galina is never at a loss.

G.V. I think it's my way of respecting my art. I would not allow myself to step on the stage without thorough preparation. I cannot tolerate carelessness, clumsiness, or compromise, either in life or in the artistic domain. In the theater, I cannot stand it when someone who doesn't look the part is allowed to play a young woman, the kind of role that is so common in Russian opera. No matter what the quality of the voice, this is intolerable and leaves the public with an uneasy feeling. This is also true for men. The theater has certain aesthetic demands which must not be treated lightly.

M.R. Galina is amazingly gifted. Having gotten her start in operetta, she championed a personal dramatic perspective in opera that earned her a special place at the Bolshoi, above the others. One can even say that she originated a new wave and a theatrical approach, which numerous articles on the Bolshoi have pointed out. Thus, when Galina was in *The Snow Maiden*, performances in which she sang not the title role but that of Kupava, it was really she who "killed" the Snow Maiden, and the critics wrote that Rimsky-Korsakov's opera should be rechristened *Kupava*.

Galina was considered a true actress, which explains her attitude with respect to the public. However, I don't entirely agree with her about physically "looking the part," since opera is an art of conventions. We know that Gigli had a big belly and short legs, but if we had never heard him sing, we would have been much the poorer for it!

G.V. Times have changed. If Gigli were to come back today in the role of Lenski, even with his divine voice, audiences would no longer accept him as they did at the beginning of the century. Before that, Figner, who created the role of Lenski, sported a beard and a moustache—which actually annoyed Tchaikovsky. Nowadays, that would be an impossible sight. The theater has new standards.

C.S. Some present-day musicians claim that formal training is useless, that teachers are good for nothing—other than, sometimes, ruining the voice—and that, in the final analysis, self-training is better. How do you feel about this?

G.V. You must be kidding! To express vocally what he feels, how can an artist pull it off unless he possesses the necessary technique? How can he do it? For someone like me, who has always sung, my vocal problems were corrected the day I met Madame Vera Garina. She was then eighty-three years old.

C.S. Who was Madame Garina?

41

G.V. She was a singer who had studied in Vienna at the turn of the century. After the Revolution, she stopped singing and devoted herself to teaching. Madame Garina was my only teacher. I am truly her creation. If it hadn't been for her, I never would have become an opera singer. I would have gone on singing music-hall songs. Though, to tell the truth, I had already had another teacher who, in six months, managed to wipe out all my high notes, which obliged me to go on the operetta stage for four years.

Madame Garina began by giving me back my high notes. She understood me and I understood her. It was a once-in-a-lifetime case of mutual compatibility between student and teacher. She devoted herself totally to my voice and allowed me to enter the Bolshoi where I became a prima donna right away. That was 1952, and Madame Garina died four years later. Because she lived in Leningrad [now St. Petersburg], she never heard me at the Bolshoi. But when I gave concerts in Leningrad, in the large Philharmonic Hall, she was right there in the front row.

C.S. Amen to the power of teaching—

G.V. Yes, as you see, no stage director, no conductor, no singer, no matter how great, can achieve the slightest results without technique. An artist might have brilliant ideas, but if he cannot manage to give them a tangible form adapted to his own instrument, whether it be vocal or purely instrumental, they're of no use. The risk is not merely ending up with a less brilliant result or wasting ten years, but in the case of a young singer, ruining the voice beyond repair.

M.R. I think Galina is right. To make an analogy, it's as if someone were to set out to invent the bicycle today. "Don't worry about the bicycle," the teacher would say, "since the motorcycle has already been invented. You could save time if you tried to build airplanes instead." Likewise, in music, a teacher imparts his own level of achievement; it's useless to waste time with the preliminaries. Then, the student is forced to find the method of attaining a superior level on his own.

Let me tell you about a personal experience. It concerns Beethoven's Cello Sonata in A major, a piece I've been playing for at least twenty-five years. Now, this sonata presents certain difficulties, specifically concerning shifting finger positions. It wouldn't be noticeable on the piano or the clarinet, but on the violoncello, it's audible. For twenty-five years I thought about the best way to achieve this change of position, and it wasn't until the last time I played it, with Pollini, that I found a marvelous solution! I discovered the exact place where it's possible to make the change!

Let's imagine that another cellist has just confronted the same problem and would likewise ponder it for twenty or thirty years before resolving it. It's obvious I should explain my solution to him immediately so he doesn't waste any more time. I would have been happy if a teacher told me what he had learned and, consequently, what I ought to do.

Furthermore, the performer must possess a wide range of knowledge, a total cultural education. How can he perform a cello concerto without being acquainted with operas and symphonies?

G.V. Your performer still might have a great education, but if he doesn't have the technique, he won't achieve anything. Even with the best of intentions, he can wear himself out if his fingers or voice don't function.

M.R. Technique is to a musician what words are to a poet. Words—everyone knows them, yet there are those who are poets and those who are not. There is one poet for every one million people— Well, musicians must work on their technique, but only one in ten thousand will become a performer. Technique is the musician's language, and thanks to

43

two God-given gifts—talent and imagination—he can transcend that language. It is always possible to develop certain qualities, but if you have nothing, nothing can be developed. If you say, "Play this note for me with sadness," a talented artist will understand you and play the note with the nuance you desire. The one who is bereft of talent will settle for making a sad face in place of the sad note.

C.S. But on what level can a teacher intervene? How can he explain what the student must do?

M.R. Personally, when I give a course for cellists, I prefer to sit at the piano so they don't copy whatever I might be doing with my cello. I'm against imitation. For a musician, the essential is to know exactly what one wants to achieve. Even before picking up the instrument, one must have something definite in mind and know the sound one wishes to produce. Then the muscles will always achieve the required miracles.

If I were asked, for example, to name the muscle that does the job and state when it functions and the pressure one should exert, I would be unable to give a precise answer, for muscle control depends, first of all, on willpower. And willpower is transformed into muscle control as when the sound of the voice is converted by the microphone into electrical current. Anyone who meticulously rationalizes every muscular pressure runs a great risk of paralysis. It's the tale of the centipede (in Russia, we say it has only forty feet). When asked, "What's your thirty-second foot doing when you advance your eighteenth?" the centipede thought a moment and ceased to move! Thereupon it replied, "I really don't know!"

I can give another example. I have to throw a projectile onto the board over there, in front of me. I aim carefully but I'm afraid I'll miss it, so I stand up and get into a more comfortable position, concentrate, aim, and hit the board. How did I do it? By the very miracle of willpower. But if I ponder over the complexity of my movements and try to find out the weight of the ball, the distance between the ball and the board—if I make all these calculations, it's possible I'll miss my target. Rationalization sometimes drags you down a dead end from which it is impossible to escape.

That's why I say to my students, "Do you know what sounds you want to produce? If your ideas are clear and your will is strong, you'll achieve good results, and your muscles will produce phenomenal feats." That's when the magic begins!

G.V. In opera, it's not enough to feel and imagine a character; it must be communicated to the audience in an immediately recognizable form. And an opera singer must possess a great technique in order to impose a sufficiently striking image with the very first notes. The audience must be able to tell right away if they're dealing with a soubrette or a queen. Now, for an artist to create a character implies a mastery of countless details. You need, at once, imagination to get under the skin of the character and the technique to externalize it. The technique must be closely linked to the expressive desire. The important thing is not necessarily what an artist-interpreter says but what he expresses. Besides, there is often a discrepancy between what one says and what one expresses, and this gap constitutes an essential element of stage histrionics. Finally, to build a character, it must be given life and credibility throughout the work as a whole. One must create a sort of bridge between the different stages of its behavior.

M.R. For my part, I have stated that, on the opera stage, singers are overburdened with clichés. They generally perform mechanical gestures that have nothing to do with their emotional state; they don't understand a word of what they're singing and don't pay the slightest attention to their partners, whose words should nevertheless inspire their own responses. In fact, a singer should listen to his partner as though he were hearing each reply for the first time in his life.

In the course of a rehearsal for *Eugene Onegin,* I tried an enlightening experiment. I chose a passage from the last act, a short, rapid dialogue between Onegin and Gremin. It's the moment when Onegin asks Gremin:

"Are you married?"

Gremin replies: "Yes."

"For a long time?"

"For two years."

"To whom?"

"To Larina."

I took the person playing Gremin aside and told him to answer, "No, I'm not married." And before we began again, I begged the one playing Onegin to pay attention.

Onegin: "Are you married?"

Gremin: "No!"

But Onegin went right on: "For how long? To whom?"

Obviously, I wouldn't dream of conducting such a test during a performance. It was simply an exercise to prove that singers, more often than not, don't listen to each other, don't hear anything, don't think about anything, and yet they respond!

G.V. No. I don't agree at all. Let's assume that Gremin replies in the negative, "No, I'm not married." What do you expect his partner to say, short of rewriting the libretto?

In opera, the parameters become different. You say one must think before answering, but one doesn't always have either the chance or the time to do that. You simply have to react spontaneously and be ready to carry on the dialogue. At any rate, great singers know how to listen!

M.R. For example, Onegin asks Lenski, "Tell me, which one is Tatiana?" But Lenski isn't listening, for at that moment he's trying to clear his voice and isn't thinking at all about his partner's question. He generally has such an oafish expression!

G.V. He probably has a frog in his throat!

M.R. That reminds me. I remember the time in New York when I played the Dvořák Concerto under the direction of George Szell. In the finale, the oboe plays a phrase which the cello then repeats. Now, the oboist had a technical problem and missed a note, but I answered him with the cello by making the same slip; George Szell, whose disposition wasn't always the most agreeable, nevertheless rewarded us with a big smile because I had returned the oboe's stray volley with my racquet.

I repeat, one must be ready to listen to others. This is my own approach to art. If one day a certain passage brought tears to my eyes, a thousand performances later, at the same place in the work, I should still feel the tears. It's not a matter of preserving the habit of weeping over that passage, but of keeping the emotion fresh. Nothing is more frightful than routine!

C.S. Can everyday life create diversion—I mean, diversify the emotions and, as a result, enrich the art of the interpreter?

M.R. Let's suppose that, for a certain time, I'm tired of life. The sight of a friend doesn't make me happy, the sadness of my neighbor doesn't touch me—in short, I become indifferent and immediately start playing worse— For me, contact with others is essential. If life doesn't bring me any emotion, I have nothing more to communicate in music.

For example, going to a party, dancing with friends, having a drink with someone, or even staying up all night—these are important restoratives for me. Through them, I can rejuvenate my emotions and have the strength to breathe these emotions back into my music. Thus, last night, I couldn't sleep; I even took a sleeping pill, but it took effect too late and I arrived totally drowsy in front of the orchestra. As soon as I saw the orchestra, however, and spotted my musician-friends and Henri Dutilleux, one of whose works I was performing, I straightened right up, pulled myself together—and I don't think I played too badly. Maybe I wouldn't have played as well if I had had a good night's sleep!

G.V. If you had slept, you would have played even better!

M.R. No, if I had slept for forty-eight hours, I wouldn't have played well!

G.V. But why would you want to sleep for forty-eight hours?

M.R. The day of a concert, if I sleep a long time in the afternoon, I cannot play well. The artist's nerves have to be on edge. When I stay up, I play well! And if I sleep and wake up too late, I play like a beast!

G.V. That's a shame!

M.R. I think that for every activity there is a specific professional physical prerequisite. For boxers, the fists are the most important, and for a mover, it's having a strong back: each profession requires its own strength. For the artist, it's getting his nervous system in shape. He has to react to the slightest events at phenomenal speed.

One day when I was in London, I attended a particularly remarkable concert by David Oistrakh. When I went to see him in his dressing room, I told him, "Today you played wonderfully." He replied, "That's because today I had the time to do everything."

What does this mean? That his nerves were so keen that he'd had the time, even during the shortest notes, to realize all his intentions. When your emotions are dulled, you let the notes go by without giving them the necessary expression.

On the other hand, there are happy moments when your muscles respond to your every desire, and that's when you have sufficient time to express the maximum emotion. That's what David Oistrakh meant.

Some artists practice yoga. I believe that's a big mistake. I probably won't live quite as long as they will, two or three days less—my profession demands sacrifices!—and coal miners or deep-sea divers will have even shorter lives. The equilibrium that yoga gives goes hand-in-hand with a contemplative attitude which, from my point of view, runs contrary to the nervous tension that a successful concert demands. Yoga practitioners may acquire the balance they seek but lose the nervous edge that the artist feeds on. Could you imagine Dostoyevsky's nervous system in a state of perfect calm?

G.V. Every person expresses himself in his own way and chooses the rhythm of his life. You have a crazy lifestyle! There are some extraordinary artists who perform infrequently and who can sleep and take their time—without it affecting their energy level!

C.S. Let's take the case of Horowitz—

M.R. Well, when he plays, his nerves are as taut and on edge as mine. I know because I've played with him. You see, it's not only because one is running from the plane to the concert hall—

G.V. But you prefer your crazy lifestyle—

M.R. I said nothing of the sort. I merely said that if I rested, I wouldn't necessarily play better!

The Interpreter's Mission

C.S. For the music lover, music is a more or less agreeable and meaningful listening experience. For the professional, music is primarily a score made up of staves, notes, and time signatures—a whole language accessible only to the initiated. What is the relation between this printed code and the sounds produced—or, to put it another way, how does musical interpretation come about?

M.R. When I read a score, I immediately hear the notes in my head, and each note has its own timbre. I consult the score as though I were reading a book, with great concentration. I need total silence. The slightest noise disturbs me, so night-time is when I'm most comfortable at it. But that's only the first step. I go on to read the score a second and then a third time while the work begins to take shape in my head. It's a mental activity prior to any contact with the instrument. This is when I study the score as a whole, when I get to know its language and try to get inside the composer's mind. I imagine how all the various parts should sound. Here, the sound might be gay or sad, warm, red-hot, brilliant, with great vibrato or relatively neutral, or it might be thick and tragic. It's a whole world which gradually grows out of the composer's wishes.

C.S. Is everything written in the score?

M.R. No, of course not. In fact, what is *not* written down is the most important thing. Reading a score and understanding it means knowing what the composer wanted to say. But each performer might receive that message differently, particularly when a work has never been played. In this respect, I've had lots of experience, having received large numbers of scores that have never been performed. I must admit that, in the beginning, I didn't always figure out the composer's intentions. When I felt my sight-reading work was finished and the result at least corresponded to what I wanted, I would be eager to submit my interpretation to the composer. It was essential for me to know if I had grasped the mood of the music I was performing. While playing, seeing the composer's face was enough indication for me to know his impressions. Then, he would make comments.

When a composer tells you, "You know, I think this movement could be played a little faster—or a little slower," it means you haven't really got it right. When that happened to me, it grieved me a lot, for I wanted to get it right 100 percent of the time! Still, as I continued working, I would manage to temper the composer's remarks.

C.S. Aren't these "remarks" in fact part of a necessary dialogue?

M.R. Indeed, and along these lines, I have a particularly curious recollection about the Shostakovich First Concerto.

When I performed the work for the first time, Shostakovich felt I had come out right all along the line, so he adopted the tempos of my interpretation for the published version of the score. However, five years later, I changed my own interpretation, specifically by speeding up the first movement, which to me seemed better suited to the spirit of the music. In any case, I considered that modification an improvement, and I think Shostakovich shared that feeling. But the "error" of my first interpretation remained in print for posterity.

C.S. Can a composer be wrong about the interpretation of his own works?

M.R. Yes, and I will even say that that is very often the case. Just as when a performer approaches the score in an abstract manner when reading it, a composer doesn't always sense right away how the work actually sounds as it's being written. When the instrumental parts are written out, the composer generally reconsiders his tempos and, more often than not, makes them faster. For, as soon as the written note becomes sound, the composer realizes the great difficulty, especially with a bow, of playing slowly. There is one exception: Olivier Messiaen. He always asked me to play slower, no matter how slow a tempo I had chosen. I must say that Messiaen is right, for if his music is played too fast, it is likely to lose its most profound qualities and essential meaning. For instrumentalists, Messiaen is really a very difficult writer, especially in the slow movements.

When I played the cello part in *Quatuor pour la fin du temps*, I dreamt of a bow which would completely surround me. One would have only to turn it and turn it nonstop, and the musical line would truly go on into infinity. First chance I get, I'm going to have a special bow built, a bow over fifty centimeters long, which would be used only for *Quatuor pour la fin du temps*!

53

C.S. Let's return to the various stages of musical performance. You begin, essentially, by mental "sight-reading"?

M.R. Indeed, but as soon as I have a general sense of the score, I grab my cello and play, play with all my passion—

But never will you hear a more revolting interpretation. I've just gone from the stage of mental interpretation to that of execution, and this first attempt is truly horrible. The technical aspect of the work is what I call execution; interpretation is style. I have the style in my mind, but I still am not able to bring it properly to life in sound. At this stage, it really sounds awful!

C.S. But nobody hears it!

M.R. No, no, they couldn't. I even hide it from my family! This is when I circle the passages containing technical difficulties I haven't mastered. And, like a surgeon, I "cut out" these parts, work on them, concentrate on certain details, and start playing all over again, trying little by little to reconcile my abstract concept with its instrumental realization. After a great deal of this tedious technical effort, I reapproach the work and try to attain the ideal I hold within me.

According to Tolstoy, music begins where speech ends. The process of musical communication is, indeed, absolutely specific. Music speaks to mankind and addresses the human heart with a particular language much more profound than the spoken word. For me, the spoken word is to music as earthly life is to life in the hereafter. The scales of values and manners of thought are different in the world beyond. For me, music remains a great mystery.

C.S. I forget what famous virtuoso told how he happened to learn a score during a flight and played it for the first time upon his arrival, during the concert. Is this possible?

M.R. It's perfectly possible. When I play, my mind gives the orders to my muscles. The most important thing is concentration, which allows one to maintain control of the fingers. Studying the score can therefore save one from a much longer fingering practice, and it's actually this mental study that gives one the means to learn a work by heart and engrave it in one's memory. One has the feeling of playing automatically because everything is already together inside the head. Playing the work five times for oneself is fine, but spending three hours with the score is even more valuable.

G.V. As for me, when I approach a work I don't know, I first work mechanically, learning the score word for word while ignoring its expressive aspect. For hours. All alone. Then, when I have a general idea of the work, I work on each phrase at length. I try to understand the reasons for an interval, a passage which isn't comfortable for the voice, and—even more—the process implemented by the composer. I can do it only when I'm alone, and I need time. Sometimes I spend an hour on one interval. And it's only when I've gone beyond this sight-reading stage and am able to enter into the spiritual world of the composer that I let my own personality express itself. My emotions complete the score just as the artist's chalks give a sketch its definitive character.

C.S. Essentially, it's an approach which is related to that of the instrumentalist.

M.R. Yes, but the voice is physically more difficult to master than the instrument. A soprano must control her breathing, test her high notes and low notes, and cannot content herself with an abstract result.

C.S. Furthermore, the opera singer must imagine a character and make it live for the audience.

G.V. To bring a character to life, it's not enough to imagine and feel it. Certain psychological states must be communicated to the audience through the use of a whole arsenal of technical possibilities. A highly temperamental artist can wail away, wring her hands, and chew the scenery—with all best intentions—and still leave the audience stone-cold. On the other hand, you sometimes get the impression that an artist is about to die of love, right there in front of you; even onstage, certain colleagues give me that feeling, but the next second they'll turn their head and tell me a joke under their breath. That's what I call supreme technique.

C.S. The idea is therefore not to be sincere but to give the illusion of being natural?

G.V. Provided that the "naturalness" is effective. Unfortunately, the trend today is toward the "pseudo-natural," as though it were enough to behave onstage as one behaves in life. Personally, I get annoyed by all those performances in which tragic actors mouth a text by Racine or Shakespeare in an utterly "natural" voice—which is to say common and vulgar. One can be natural in one's kitchen, but it's not a particularly desirable quality on a stage; after all, the art of the theater is above and beyond everyday existence, and the artist must enter into that other life.

Now, to give the illusion of naturalness, the artist must possess fabulous technical mastery! Of course he has to be sincere, but without technique, sincerity has no meaning. Technique allows you to touch the audience by bridging the physical distance between the stage and the auditorium; technique transforms the ordinary voice into one that makes an audience sit up and listen; technique gives theater a grandeur that it tends to lose through the effects of film and television. And this statement is just as valid for modern works as it is for the classical repertoire.

C.S. You—like Slava—have wide experience in the field of contemporary music, having often had the opportunity, both in Russia and in the West, to sing works composed with you in mind. What type of collaboration can a performer have with a composer, and to what extent can an artist actually influence a composer's work?

G.V. I've collaborated notably with Shostakovich and Benjamin Britten, but to say that I gave my point of view in order to influence their creative work would be exaggerating. Before Britten composed the *War Requiem,* an important solo part of which was written for me, he had attended one of my recitals at the Aldeburgh Festival. That evening I sang arias from Bellini's *Norma* and from *Fidelio,* followed by some romances by Tchaikovsky, and ending with Mussorgsky's *Songs and Dances of Death.* It really was an absolutely mad program. It was the first time that Britten heard me, and I think that concert had an important influence on the vocal writing of my part in the *War Requiem.* It seems to me I recognize passages in the *Requiem* that contain very wide intervals and that could have been written by Mussorgsky. In other places, Britten's writing reminds me of the Italian style. It all reveals the impression he got from that concert. It was following that recital that Benjamin Britten came backstage to tell me that he wanted to write for me.

As far as Shostakovich is concerned, I recall the concert during which I sang the world premiere of *Satires,* the cycle on a text by Sacha Chorny that he had written for me and dedicated to me. In the first half, I sang *Songs and Dances of Death,* which he later orchestrated for me and, again, dedicated to me. That's what led him to compose the Symphony No. 14, and the impression made by that Mussorgsky-Shostakovich evening constitutes the distant though direct inspiration for that work. This is one way a singer can have an influence on a composer.

That said, Shostakovich would never make any comments to his performers. You had to figure things out for yourself, which made it difficult to master the complexity of his music.

M.R. May I finish Galina's answer? The question is, to what extent can a performer help a composer? It's obvious in the case of Shostakovich or Britten that there was nothing to change. But there are cases when Galina informed composers of her wishes. For example, when Marcel Landowski showed her his score as he was working on it, she asked him to write it in a higher tessitura, and he took that remark into consideration.

G.V. Yes, all this is true when a performer has the chance to work with a composer. But Shostakovich never revealed his works until they were finished. Landowski, on the other hand, showed me his score when it had barely been started, so we were able to work together.

C.S. It's a sharing of responsibilities?

G.V. In some cases, it's a rather unusual type of collaboration. Indeed, a composer may happen to have, from the very beginning, quite a specific idea for his composition; in that case, the performer's input can neither disturb him nor drive him in another direction. Another composer may prefer to collaborate with performers from the very start, most likely because he has less knowledge of their artistic capabilities.

M.R. It all depends on the composer with whom you're working. I'll tell you about the experiences I had with two great Russian composers: Shostakovich and Prokofiev. Only once did Shostakovich show me a score before it was completed; it was the Second Cello Concerto, and for one particular passage, I gave him a little idea: "Here, it would sound better if the fourths were played together." Now, at the time, the cadenza hadn't been composed, so imagine my surprise and delight when I saw the finished cadenza and noticed that he had taken my suggestion. That said, I'd add that Shostakovich wasn't interested in technique for technique's sake.

With Prokofiev, it was a different story. He would ask your opinion of each note, each bar, but it couldn't be you who went to him with a question! On certain days, when he was bored or simply wanted to see me, he would phone me and say, "Slava, I have something for you. Come quickly!" As soon as I'd arrive, he would show me one bar: "What do you think of it? Will it sound good?" The technical aspect of composition fascinated him. Sometimes he would write music like others work crossword puzzles. From time to time, he would tell me, "Here, play me a rapid passage on the cello— anything at all, as long as it's fast." You can imagine how I'd put my mind to it, all the more since I had taken some composition courses. So, I would offer a passage in which I tried to match his own style and really give my very best. In that two-bar passage, there may have been as many as sixty-four notes! He would look at the passage in silence, think about it, concentrate, cross out something, then pick up a little eraser, get rid of one of the sixty-four notes, and replace it with another note. By then I'd be ready to jump out the window, because it would be precisely that new note which added the touch of genius to the passage. And I'd wonder, Why couldn't *I* find the right note? One note in sixty-four was enough to make the difference between an ungifted lout and a genius! Prokofiev liked to work in this somewhat experimental manner, and nothing could disturb him.

Another day, I arrived at Prokofiev's and said to him, "Look at this melody line for the cello; it climbs so high that the sound becomes terribly pinched. Would it be possible to lower the second theme of the first movement by two octaves?" He sat down at the piano, looked at me, and began to play: "Don't you think it's easier to have the accompaniment low and the melody high?" Confronted by my look of doubt, he continued with an expletive, then: "Young man, don't you see you're bothering me?" I left feeling very upset over my blunder; I had said what shouldn't have been said because I might, naturally enough, have played the theme in the upper register with a grating tone. But that evening, Prokofiev called me up (and I must say that he rarely called me): "Slava, without my tremendous technique as a composer, I wouldn't have been able to carry out your stupid proposal!" And he hung up! In fact, Prokofiev had completely changed the accompaniment and, in the place of a very simple formula, had dreamt up a lacy scoring for string pizzicatos and woodwind staccatos.

C.S. Have any composers insisted that you perform things you didn't want to do?

G.V. No, never.

M.R. Sometimes, bad composers oblige us to play bad works!

G.V. I recall the day at the Bolshoi when I was forced to sing an opera by Muradeli called *October*. It was the most humiliating experience of my life! I, who had never agreed to make the slightest compromise, stepped onto the stage saying to myself, God, when can I leave? I'm so ashamed!

M.R. She forbade me to attend the performance. It's the only role of Galina's I never heard her sing.

G.V. I was really compelled to do it by Madame Furtseva [then Soviet minister of culture]; if I had refused, I might never have been able to perform abroad again. Lenin was one of the characters in the opera, and so of course the opera had to be championed by the greatest artists of the Bolshoi.

Madame Furtseva had told me, "At least sing the premiere because the entire government will be in the auditorium. Then you can drop the role if you want, I don't care!"

C.S. And it was really that bad?

G.V. It was worthless! Something totally devoid of musical quality, on a kindergarten level. I have never understood how Muradeli could have been included on the list of formalists, alongside composers like Shostakovich and Prokofiev.

M.R. It was truly a great stroke of luck for him!

G.V. Right after the decree of 1948 condemning his opera *The Great Friendship*, he went around shouting, "I'm not a formalist! I am an honest Communist! It was purely by accident that I ended up on that list with Shostakovich. I had nothing to do with it." And to prove it, he wrote some folk songs and that opera on Lenin! It was horrible!

C.S. When I asked if any composers made you do something that went against your own wishes, I was thinking less about the political constraints you had in the Soviet Union than about problems posed by ultra-modern trends. I was thinking particularly about avant-garde composers, who are said to mistreat the voice or who write "against the instrument."

G.V. Those problems exist, but in order to resolve them, it's sometimes merely a matter of willpower and practice. I'll tell you what happened to me with the Penderecki *Te Deum*, which was supposed to premiere in the United States. One day, Slava called me up and said, "Listen, you must be in this premiere, you have to accept it. It's easy. It's more or less like the Verdi *Requiem*. It's written for the pope and doesn't pose any major difficulties. It's between forty and sixty minutes long. There are four soloists. You simply must do it."

Very well! I receive the score, and it reminds *me* of the Verdi *Requiem* too. Not to worry, I have plenty of time! But two weeks before the concert, when I opened the score, I saw I was in trouble! It was terribly difficult. If it hadn't been for Slava, I would have thrown a scarf around my neck and declared myself indisposed, and that would have been the end of it! I never would have made the premiere! Well, I didn't leave my piano for twelve days. In the beginning, I didn't understand a thing; for ten days I hadn't the foggiest idea what I was doing. But when I began to comprehend, I realized that it was a work of grandeur, and that my part was the most interesting one in it. In fact, I had some rather free-style phrases to sing where I could change the accents and make the whole thing my own. In the end, Penderecki told me he was very pleased, and I was happy too.

C.S. So the performer's best asset is the gradual realization that transforms a strange land into familiar territory?

M.R. On this subject, too, I have an interesting story to tell concerning Prokofiev. After the doctors told him he couldn't go out at night, he turned it to his own advantage by composing, especially when he wasn't able to fall asleep. But while composing, he would doze off, and as soon as he woke up in the morning he would rush to the piano to play what he had written the night before. "When I start to play," he told me, "I think, My God, how could I have written such a silly thing and think it was interesting? It'll keep me from sleeping tonight!" Then he would play the same passage a second time and think, "No, after all, it isn't all that bad! And when I play it a third time I think it's really what I had to write!" Yes, Prokofiev actually told me this secret. It means that a composer sometimes may not appreciate his own score—or, at any rate, not immediately. I'd say that it was dictated to him by divine inspiration, and when he rereads it the next day, after the inspiration has gone, he no longer understands what he wanted to say. Yet after going over the piece again and again, he gets back to the original inspiration.

All the composers I have known worked every day, like factory workers. And Shostakovich, who had a portrait of Mussorgsky on his desk and a wastebasket under the table, would tell me while staring at the portrait, "When I look at those eyes of his, it helps me to throw my works into the basket." He had a tremendous musical conscience, because he was able to fill the wastebasket with his own music!

C.S. In a chapter about performing, we're speaking mostly about composers, which is to be expected; but we're sticking to the contemporary field, which is less so. In fact, the performer's daily bread is the classical repertoire. Slava, when you conduct a symphony by Beethoven or Brahms for the first time, can you ignore the great masters who conducted it before you?

M.R. Absolutely. And I must ignore them. The truth is inscribed in the score, and studying it closely allows interesting discoveries to be made. I'll give you a specific example, which is a bit technical but which proves you can never read a score too many times. While studying the First Symphony of Brahms, I noticed that, at letter E in the first movement, the first and second violins, for eight bars, play a less important role than the violas, cellos, and double basses. Now, all five parts bear the same marking, *fortissimo,* but if they play with the same intensity, the high instruments are going to cover the low instruments; so, to prevent the theme from being buried, Brahms put dots over the violins' eighth notes, but not over the ones for violas, cellos, and double basses. That made me think that the eighth notes for the three low voices should be longer than the ones for the violins, though in all the performances I know they have exactly the same value. Giving different lengths to those eighth notes sets the theme in relief and emphasizes the counterpoint in the first and second violins. Brahms made no mistake in not putting dots over all the notes in these few bars, but only a close analysis of the score showed me why. This is my own discovery; I didn't make it by listening to other interpretations, and I haven't encountered it anywhere else.

C.S. Galina, when you do a role for the first time, can you ignore what other singers have done with it?

G.V. When I'm learning a role, I never listen to recordings. Only when I have mastered the role and my voice has reached the very last stages of polishing it do I sometimes listen to recordings by good sopranos, but not as a rule. I don't want to be influenced by another interpretation before having a clear idea of the character. When I am onstage, I must first express my own personality, but sometimes another interpretation might have something interesting to contribute to mine.

When I started to sing Mussorgsky, I hadn't heard any other interpretations, and when I studied *Songs and Dances of Death*, it was as though I had received a score on the very day it had been written. I was singing and creating my style of interpretation. Twenty years later, in 1981, when I gave a master course in Aldeburgh, I heard for the first time someone else sing Mussorgsky's cycle; it was quite disconcerting to me, for I had gotten used to my own interpretation.

C.S. Does singing a repertory piece without ever having heard it mean you turn your back on tradition?

G.V. What one calls tradition is often a false tradition. At some point, one loses track of whose tradition it is and, even more so, of how it became established. False traditions mostly affect very well-known works. Such is the case with the "Tchaikovsky tradition," which is a great misfortune for singers. The original message has been buried beneath layers of sentimentality. By peeling away these layers and approaching the music as though it were new, one gets back to the score in its original purity.

C.S. What is meant by "getting back to the style of the composer"?

G.V. I don't know, and it doesn't interest me. What does the "Schubert tradition" mean, other than singers imitating each other and modeling their vocal phrasing on that of a famous colleague? It's so simple to mimic. You merely need to listen to a good singer's records for a couple of hours. But it isn't interpretation. Now, every true artist has his own personality and, sometimes involuntarily, breathes it into his own performance. The truthfulness of the interpretation lies in that.

C.S. But that truthfulness is dated. What I mean is, an interpretation is connected to a point in time.

G.V. Everything in life changes: people, techniques, behavior, and musical interpretation. One cannot expect singers to sound like they did at the turn of the century; it wouldn't be possible, or even tolerable. Our souls are filled with a spirit suited to our era. We wear denim and circle the globe in a few hours. Our nervous systems react differently, we relate to the world around us in new ways. One must not overlook that truth, for music is a living thing. It is created by and for living human beings. This also goes for the handing down of music of the past—music which was, in its own time, very much alive.

Take Bach, for example. He was a robust individual who liked to drink and eat, and who had I don't know how many children. He put all of himself into his compositions. Musicians must bring their own vitality to the music of Bach when they play it today. They shouldn't be content with practicing in order to attain some sort of celestial disembodiment.

C.S. Slava, when you play the Bach Suites for Unaccompanied Cello, are you concerned with getting as close as possible to what Bach's contemporaries might have heard?

M.R. We obviously have an idea about this. For example, we're familiar with the type of fortepiano Beethoven used and know that that very imperfect instrument underwent considerable technical improvements before becoming the perfect instrument we presently have. But I'd also remind you that cars powered by steam engine existed prior to today's vehicles; it would never occur to anyone to return to manufacturing the slower-moving prototype. Our superb modern pianos are precisely the ones which best embody Beethoven's ideas. If someone today were to make a cello whose capacity for volume could be extended without affecting the quality and variety of the timbre, I would immediately start practicing on the new instrument and use *it* to play the Bach Suites. In today's huge concert halls seating three or four thousand, the sound must reach each listener without difficulty.

One day at a rehearsal, when the horns were having problems, Shostakovich told me, "*I* won't live long enough, but *you* may still be around when they invent infallible horns." It's already obvious that today's horns are better than the ones we used to have, but you cannot keep me from hoping that tomorrow's will be even more superior. No doubt, a few "specialists" will still call for those faulty old horns that Haydn and Beethoven wrote for. That's the best way to achieve more flaws and to hear more bad notes.

C.S. I'm not completely convinced. Naturally there are cases of indisputable technical improvements for instruments like the horn or the harp. But there are also specific sounds that have long been forgotten and which some musicians are now trying to recapture in the name of authenticity. For example, I'm thinking of the harpsichord which, in a Brandenburg Concerto or in a Mozart opera, has fortunately replaced the usurping piano.

M.R. That's a different matter, when the instrument is truly different. I didn't compare the harpsichord with the piano. I compared two different types of pianos, such as the Hammerklavier and the modern Steinway. Likewise, I'm comparing the old horn with the contemporary horn, the viola da gamba with the cello. Obviously, modern instruments must not be used unless they have an analogous sonority. Moreover, did the composers write for the instrument they had at their disposal, or rather for an ideal instrument? Bach is a genius, whose music has continued to be heard for more than two centuries, but the viola da gamba didn't last two hundred years. Bach's ideas were in advance of an instrument whose makeup was still very primitive.

C.S. Have you tried playing the Bach Suites on a viola da gamba?

M.R. Yes, I have tried, but I soon gave up. That said, I'd also like to mention the problem of instrumental balance. It's obvious that the viola da gamba sounds better with the harpsichord than the cello, because the harpsichord is a more intimate instrument and the sound of the cello tends to overwhelm it. Better balance is achieved when the viola da gamba is played with the harpsichord. Putting a viola da gamba with a piano would produce a comic effect—

In any case, as I said a short time ago, the truth is inscribed in the scores. One need only study them in order to know what the composer wanted. Thus, one can understand that the Brandenburg Concertos, sometimes played by a large orchestra, were intended for a solo ensemble. It is inherent in

67

the music. The Ninth Symphony appears to have been played in Beethoven's time by a modest-size orchestra. But do you really believe that Beethoven, if he were alive today, would be averse to a performance of his Ninth with 250 instrumentalists, choristers, and soloists combined?

As regards musical performance, there is no definitive truth. With Beethoven, the important thing is not the technical improvement of one instrument or another, but the effect of his music on the listener. Beethoven was a genius because he expressed feelings which never fade.

Here is another convincing argument: today, the plays of Shakespeare are performed the world over, and directors treat them in totally different ways—but every performance is able to move us with what remain identifiable emotions and situations, which ultimately go back to the genius of Shakespeare. I imagine that productions in Shakespeare's time were entirely different, and I'm sure it would be futile for anyone to set about restoring the Elizabethan theatrical style, for we have another style of life, another way of perceiving history. But it's the timeless ideas and emotions that remain the same. Five hundred years ago, didn't jealousy exist? And love? And crime and terrorism, too— Composers able to communicate these emotions address the entire world and go far beyond the boundaries of so-called nationalistic schools. They claim that Russians are sentimental and willingly wear their hearts on their sleeves, that the French are seducers, that the Germans harness the force of their ideas, that each nationality possesses specific traits. In Russia, we had some remarkable composers who precisely translated certain national characteristics into music: Arensky or Kalinnikov, for example. They are typically Russian. As for Mussorgsky, Tchaikovsky, Stravinsky, Prokofiev, or Shostakovich, although they are Russian, they attained such a lofty level in their art that they form a part of a universal heritage.

The message of Beethoven is universal, too. It translates

the great emotions shared by the whole of humanity and expresses eternal values. The worst criminal cries when he suffers and smiles when he is happy. These God-created impulses are universally experienced. Beethoven? For me, he is Russian, as is Bach and Shakespeare. Because I, who am Russian, am deeply affected by what they express.

Furthermore, as a Russian, should I have some sort of priority in performing the cello concertos that Shostakovich wrote for me, dedicated to me, and heard me play a hundred times? Well, when I was on the jury of the Tchaikovsky Competition, I listened to young musicians from all over the world play those works, and some of their interpretations gave me remarkable ideas. Yes, they are Russian works, yet so international! Likewise, Furtwängler's example provided me with the most important tools for interpreting Tchaikovsky.

C.S. It seems to me, however, that the notion of universality in music contains some weaknesses. Are we able to hear, with the truth of its intent, the traditional music of Vietnam or Java? Will a Vietnamese musician share our emotion after hearing Beethoven's Fifth Symphony? Experience would seem to prove the contrary.

M.R. I'd answer you by saying that, in the field of boxing, there are different categories, determined according to weight. A ninety-pound weakling doesn't get into the ring with a two-hundred-pound heavyweight. So don't use people from different musical cultures as an example. Some people have primitive music and haven't attained a certain musical level.

I'll give a different example. A very great painter, whose name I withhold, cannot tell the difference between Haydn and Mozart. One evening during dinner, after a concert in which I had in fact played some Haydn, he said to me, "Slava, I'll never forget your Mozart!"

"Yes, but unfortunately I played Haydn!"

A half-hour later, he continued: "I didn't much like the music of the young composer you played, but your Mozart was fantastic!"

He hadn't heard or understood a thing! Some highly intelligent people can go to a concert—and get nothing out of it!

C.S. Imagine that you're playing the Bach Suites in a little village deep in the heart of Asia. Would you be able to find listeners who could appreciate this music?

M.R. No, because I know very well that the musical culture of that village has not yet attained that level.

A long time ago, I traveled all over Russia with my cello and an accordionist, giving concerts. Sometimes I would arrive in a village where they had never seen a real-life musician. But, when I was among the villagers, a circle would form around me, and I'd tell them all about the instruments—how a cello was made, the type of wood used—and when I told them that my cello was two hundred years old, I would hear a long sigh: "Aaahhh!"

At first, they surely believed I was lying to them. I then explained to them what a nocturne was and played one by Tchaikovsky. I would gradually pull them into the music so they'd want to know more about it. If I had started by playing a Bach Suite, it would have been like giving an aspirin tablet to a cancer patient. I would have scared them away from the music, and they would have thought, "This isn't really interesting. He's moving his arm, he's scraping something, but who knows why."

C.S. So the interpreter is a sort of missionary?

M.R. Absolutely! With my orchestra in Washington, I hope we can take grand tours all over the United States, hitting the

70

small towns and bypassing the cities that are already lucky enough to have a large orchestra. For the farmers, I wouldn't choose to conduct Ives but works likely to please at first hearing. There are still so many places where we can be pioneers! And we have to take enough time to accomplish this work and to reach all kinds of audiences. A moment ago, I spoke of the universality of music, but I'm quite sure that even in Germany I could find a person who doesn't understand Beethoven!

Icons and *Kulichi*

C.S. Now let's talk about your Russian background. Your childhood, for example—

M.R. Russia, for me, is above all my family. It was the first air I breathed, my native soil, the first ground my feet touched and, obviously, the parents with whom I lived. The beauty of the Russian landscape is another story. People are quick to say the Russian outdoors is extraordinarily beautiful, but I don't entirely share that point of view. I've visited many countries, and I must say that certain regions of Switzerland, Canada, and the United States are beautiful enough to rival those of Russia. The Russians often say: "Oh, our country is the most beautiful in the world!" That's because they've never seen anything else. We even have a song that goes: "Bulgaria is a beautiful land, but the most beautiful of all is Russia." One might also add that it depends on the period of your life— Looking back, there is a certain period of my

73

life—from 1969 to 1974—that I could have skipped altogether! It evokes only bad memories for me, although it was a splendid preparation for the happiness that I now have in the West.

C.S. What side of Russia did you experience as a child, urban or rural life?

M.R. The Russia of the cities. In summertime, we would go to the country for a few months. I remember the countryside, but even more the cities.

G.V. I remember the Russia of the cities too, Leningrad in particular. It was my native city, though I spent my childhood in Kronstadt, a fortress town built under Peter the Great, not far from Leningrad. It was both a port and a military naval base.

C.S. Your childhood memories are of Kronstadt?

G.V. Yes. You always carry your childhood inside you, thinking of it as a place you haven't visited for a long time. Quite often, people who return to a place after a long absence are disappointed by what they see. I'd prefer not to relive my childhood, though I've held on to a few good memories.

C.S. The bad memories are of the war?

G.V. I lived through the siege of Leningrad *in* Leningrad and Kronstadt. My parents hardly took care of me, so I was raised by my grandmother, who died during the siege. She died of hunger and of burns suffered when her dress caught fire. I was there. After she died, I was all alone. The siege lasted nine hundred days, and of course the schools were closed during that time.

C.S. Later on, you got to know the Russian countryside.

G.V. Yes, I know the Russian wilds and the little towns because when I started working at seventeen and went on my first tours with an operetta troupe, I crossed the country and went through all those little towns. I got my start singing jazz during the war. At fourteen or fifteen, I was already performing in public. Accompanied by a navy jazz combo, I would sing for the sailors in Kronstadt. Obviously it wasn't the jazz of today, but there were some cute songs. Then, when I was seventeen, I began singing operetta. The Germans were retreating, so we'd follow on the heels of the Russian army giving shows for the soldiers. It was a small company of thirty or forty people. When I auditioned, I was asked, "Do you want to sing anything in particular?" So I sang a romance by Rimsky-Korsakov. I was young, good-looking, and had a pretty voice, so I was hired.

I started out as one of the extras. Then, one evening, a singer fell ill and I took her role, the soubrette part, which required me to sing as well as dance. That's how my career got started, by singing Kálmán's *Mademoiselle Nitouche* [*Miss Springtime*] and *Paris in Spring,* or even Russian operettas like those of Strelnikov, the composer of *The Wedding at Malinovka.* I stayed with the operetta troupe for four years and played in as many as twenty-seven shows in one month! For four years! Those were precious years for the experience they gave me, but difficult and painful ones. Later on, those provincial tours haunted me like a nightmare. I was afraid. Afraid of traveling, afraid of hotels and those frightful restaurants, afraid of the abject poverty of those unfortunate people! At that time, the situation was the same in cities large and small. I truly dreaded tours, and when I entered the Bolshoi, I went to great lengths to avoid them. Sometimes, however, I'd be given orders: "The minister of culture demands it, Madame. You must go and sing in such-and such a place." And the concert would cost me a great deal of effort.

How can one admire the beauty of the Russian countryside while ignoring those who live there in all that poverty, a poverty that only feeds the aggression of an embittered populace?

M.R. Obviously. Such thoughts strike one as strange, here, in Paris, where you can do anything. You can walk down the street, go in a café, to the restaurant, dine with friends. Over there, in the Soviet Union, everything is difficult. You have to wait two hours before you can enter a restaurant. And you still aren't assured of finding something good! When you've finally been seated, you're surrounded by people standing and waiting their turn. Yet, one of the good things that comes from such difficulties is the birth of friendships. It's a unique characteristic of that country. Without that foundation of genuine friendship, life would be totally unbearable.

I personally like the Armenians a lot, for they have played a very important part in my life. When I was six or seven and newly arrived in Moscow with my parents and sister, we were on the street. A strange woman then came up to us; my father told her he came from Bakou and had a musically talented little boy. The woman said, "Fine. I have two rooms and there are only three of us. So we can live in one room and give you four the other room." She was Armenian, and we lived for two years with her.

G.V. For free!

M.R. She shared everything she had with us. Later, when I went on tours, I especially enjoyed my trips to Armenia, for the people there are exceptionally hospitable. Whenever my friends there came to pick me up, even before driving me to my hotel, they would insist on opening a bottle of their cognac, which they were very proud of. They claim it's as good as French cognac, but it's like the landscape: they think

Armenian cognac is excellent because they've never had French cognac! So, we'd get drunk on that cognac, and my friends and I were so happy to see each other again that I would have to make a superhuman effort to arrive at the concert hall more or less sober. My Armenian friends would have given me all they had!

In Russia, such friendship is truly precious and helps one through many difficulties. It would seem funny if you had phoned Galina this morning to tell her, "Oh, Galina, listen: I've just been to the store and picked you up six pounds of potatoes," but in Russia, it's impossible to live any other way. If nobody helps you or calls you up to say he's found something for you in a shop, it's unlivable. You knew that type of situation and faced the same difficulties during the war, but in our country, it lasts a lifetime.

C.S. How can Westerners understand the behavior of the Soviet population?

M.R. That's a delicate question. Our life is such that one definitely has to "fake it," muddle through, and fool everyone. Though no one is fooling anybody, and everyone knows it. There is a sort of general complicity. You go into the street and shout, "Long live the Communist Party!" Nobody believes you, but everybody thinks it's perfectly all right to say it, that it has to be said. Lies are forgiven. Lies are a means of survival.

Let's suppose, in spite of the love you have for your own people and your unconditional devotion toward them, that you aren't in agreement with the government. What can you do? You have two children who are still young, and when those children are seventeen and want to be accepted into the university, they'll already have a suspect reputation. And that's when the questions begin. Can one blame the father who says, "I love my children so much that I'm going to make a public declaration and cry *mea culpa*"? I am certain, and

77

Galina knows it, that the life of Shostakovich would have been different if he hadn't had two children that he loved infinitely.

So, when your children go off to school, you think about all that. You know that when they get their degrees, your children will have to submit to the decision of a commission. If the commission asks them to sign a two-year engagement to work in a distant town, it's a risk. In fact, if they leave Moscow, they'll be crossed off the city lists. Then, when they want to get back on them, they'll no longer be able to if it is known that their father or a member of their family has made any "waves." That's the reason for all the lies, lies that everyone accepts and considers normal.

G.V. Ultimately you stop thinking of them as lies. They are a part of daily life.

C.S. Can one ask the man in the street to be a hero?

M.R. There are very few heroes. And the whole population lives the lie together. Here's a little story they tell: a professor is giving a lecture on politics. He knows he is lying, and the audience knows he is lying. The audience knows *he* knows he's lying, and *he* knows the *audience* knows that he knows he's lying, and so on.

C.S. What is left today of the old Russia? Books, architecture, music—

M.R. Yes, but all that isn't as important as reshaping minds. Thus, prior to the Revolution, religion played a tremendous role in educating the children, and even in their musical training, for youngsters in the country would sing in church. Now, the people are afraid to go to church. I can give you a specific example. In 1975, two students who were in their last year of studies at the Conservatory were expelled; someone denounced them for having sung in a church. A year later, one of the two was reenrolled. Why? Because he declared, "I am guilty and understand my error, religion is nonsense, I was just ill and in a fog, now I see it all, I was wrong—"

C.S. Did your parents give you a religious education?

M.R. I remember we didn't dare bring a Christmas tree into the house before the war, for it was forbidden. I recall how at night, in secret, we'd bring in a very small pine tree wrapped in a piece of drapery, pretending to be carrying brooms. But I didn't know what religion was before I experienced a particular feeling on my own, and that was well after I had completed my studies at the Conservatory.

C.S. And Galina, what did the Church mean to you?

G.V. What do you expect it to mean to a child who is not brought up in that atmosphere? Nevertheless, I'll tell you an interesting story about my own children. There were some icons in my bedroom at home, but even though we are believers, we didn't give our children any religious instruction. Now one day, when she was six years old, my daughter Elena went to church all by herself—yes, all alone—to have the *kulichi* blessed, the traditional Easter pastry. She put on a scarf, tying it under her chin like she had seen little old ladies do, placed the *kulichi* in a napkin, and went to the church across the street, to have them blessed. The day before, on Good Friday, she had knelt at the tomb of Christ and come back home quite content.

M.R. Before the Revolution, life in Russia was very closely tied to the Church. Children would look forward to Easter because parents would plan a big celebration; there would be a great deal of activity in the home with many guests. But I never experienced anything like that. Now, you only read about it in books.

G.V. What would be the sense of a religious education nowadays? From kindergarten on, one becomes formally accustomed to lying; it's absolutely normal and essential to lie! Slava wasn't as close to our children as I because he traveled a lot. But I saw what went on with my own eyes. In school, they would be given writing assignments. Subject: the Communist Party and children. To a child of nine! What do you expect her to write about the Communist Party? So, she lies! Olga was best at it; she would write absolutely phenomenal compositions, filling entire pages. Her pen flowed nonstop, and the school has, no doubt, preserved her essays. I'd ask her, "Whatever can you be writing?" She'd burst out laughing and continue to fill page after page! She always got the best grades.

M.R. At that time there was a rather popular television program called *Animal Life* whose main character was a hare. My story takes place in a country school where the children weren't very advanced but watched a lot of television. Now, the teacher wanted to liven up her class, so when she saw a dead hare on the side of the road, she picked it up and brought it to her students.

"Tell me, children, what kind of animal is this?"

The first one answered: "A fox!"

"No, I don't think so. Anyone else?"

Another one ventured: "A wolf!"

"Hush, you silly! Don't you ever watch television? You see this fellow there every day!"

"But it *couldn't* be Lenin!"

G.V. By the time they're eleven, children have to know the constitution of the Soviet Union, by heart! The rights of man! Freedom of speech! Freedom of the press! Freedom of religion! The self-determination of the Republics! The children learn it all by heart, but even those who receive high grades don't believe a word of it. Look at China and those people who memorized Mao's little red book: it was an absolute repeat of what had occurred in Russia in the 1930s.

C.S. You seem to think of your Russian nationality on two different levels: an imaginary Russian life, from books and secondhand memories, and on the other hand, the daily reality that you have lived.

M.R. That's perfectly correct, and it represents a very rich personal experience. To give another example, I'll tell you about the first trip I took to the West in 1956. I was well acquainted with French literature, particularly Hugo, Maupassant, and Zola, who are very popular in Russia—perhaps more so than in France—and whose works I had read in translation. Thanks to those books, I had an idea of the Parisian streets, churches, the quays along the Seine. I thought, Is the reality going to match the descriptions in the novels? As a Russian, I always had a double perception: one imagined, the other based on what I saw. And when I arrived in Paris, how happy I was to see that they matched!

C.S. Do you think the great Russian tradition has been preserved in the arts?

M.R. Talents don't just disappear. Today there are still some geniuses at work in the Soviet Union, people who work clandestinely, nurturing the hope that their works will know better days, that they are just waiting to be discovered later on.

I am sure our culture is giving rise to new Dostoyevskys, but I think the constraints of life in the Soviet Union keep the number of talented people down.

C.S. Let's talk about Dostoyevsky. To the French, he represents the essence of the Russian soul. What do Russians think of him?

M.R. The Russians agree with you. Every Russian sees something of himself in Dostoyevsky.

C.S. More than in Tolstoy?

M.R. Yes, I think so. His psychology is closer to ours, closer to our crazy system, because he predicted the system; he predicted it all: how our society would function and what it would become. Tolstoy, on the other hand, speaks of the other life, the one which became our second, imaginary life. Dostoyevsky is a visionary and Tolstoy an imaginary. Tolstoy represents the old Russia, while Dostoyevsky announces the future.

C.S. And Chekhov?

M.R. Chekhov is very refined, but, to me, a bit less Russian, strange as that may seem. He's closer to Turgenev, above all in his plays. It's a bit like the music of Tchaikovsky. When you listen to it, it sounds very Russian, but when you listen to Mussorgsky, you realize which is the more Russian of the two.

C.S. What kinds of books do you ordinarily read?

M.R. We devour anything that is banned in Russia. We never stop reading and discovering new authors.

G.V. We are obviously very interested in new literature. But last year, we reread *Crime and Punishment* and found that our identification with Dostoyevsky had completely changed. It was a rereading but, nevertheless, Slava and I were literally pulling the book out of each other's hands! Dostoyevsky and Tolstoy are authors one should never stop going back to.

C.S. When did you discover the works of Dostoyevsky?

M.R. I read them when I was young and understood nothing. You read when you're fourteen, and you read again later on. When I was fourteen, my parents kept a close eye on what I read; I remember when I was at my godmother's in Orenburg, I discovered Maupassant's *Une vie* in a barn, translated in Russian. I had heard that Maupassant was a somewhat risqué writer, even quite risqué, so I picked up the book and started reading it. When my mother surprised me, she tore the book from my hands: "Never let me see you with this book again!" But I found where she had hidden it, ripped off the cover, and pasted the cover of another book in its place. When my mother approached, the title no longer gave me away. I read it all. But with the original cover I was forbidden to read Maupassant!

C.S. Beyond the political issue and, notably, in the area of artistic creation, what is it that makes the Russian artist specifically Russian?

M.R. I'm going to give you a very clear answer. When I began playing the cello thirty years ago, there was a very great difference between the French, Russian, and German schools. For example, the French would play with a very short endpin and with raised elbows. The Germans placed the elbow in another manner, and the Russians played in yet another way. Today there is no difference, because we all watch television and listen to recordings, and because even we Russians are beginning to get around. With air travel, the boundaries are vanishing.

In Russia, the phenomenon is still limited. One isn't very well informed about what goes on in the West. When the

Bolshoi Ballet came to Paris for the first time, it caused quite a stir. Why? Because its traditions were preserved in a cocoon and allowed the splendor of the past to be recaptured. Then the Bolshoi came back one year, two years, ten years later with the same artists, the same staff, similar productions. Nothing had changed. So, it was less of a success, which is absolutely understandable. Soviet artists, confined to their universe, are not invigorated by outside influences.

Today, if there is a premiere at the Opéra which interests me, and I'm in another country, I take the first flight to Paris. If I feel like seeing Béjart or Roland Petit, I go! In Russia, the possibility of such journeys does not exist. In the past, in a time when, lacking the means of communication, Russia appeared isolated, there was in fact an open, traveling elite, and fertile relations had taken root, beginning with Voltaire and Catherine the Great. Before that, Peter the Great had invited the Dutch masters. Catherine tried to transplant Western culture. What did it give us? Among other things, the potato! Yes, I believe it was she who brought us the potato on a return trip from America, and the peasants protested—

For music, I'll mention Tchaikovsky's fondness for Grieg, and the interest he took in French music and in the ballets of Léo Delibes. He used the celesta, which is a French instrument. He speaks of it in a letter: "I have heard a divine instrument." He was the first Russian composer to use it.

C.S. In spite of Western influences, Russian composers have nevertheless preserved a specific style, which is particularly noticeable in opera and other vocal music.

G.V. I'll say first of all that Russian opera is musical drama, and most of the works in the repertoire are tied to Russian history. To better sustain the drama and intensify the vocal expression, Russian composers have applied distinctive technical means which, in any case, clearly distinguish them

84

from the Western schools—and in particular from Italian composers. The vocal line hovers more in the middle register, an additional cause of fatigue for the singer. For their climaxes, Italians write a very high note, and that's what makes it expressive. Nothing of the sort for the Russians, who place the expressive passages in mid-register and often constrain performers to force their voice and display a very powerful sound. In Mussorgsky, for example, the problem for the singer is to handle the tessitura without being covered by the orchestra. For his part, Tchaikovsky very rarely uses the high register; there is only one high B-flat in Tatiana's Letter Scene, and the scene is twenty minutes long. Naturally, it's close to the character of recitative, which in Russian opera is more developed and vocally intense than in Italian opera. Finally, another difficulty about Russian opera is the potential importance of apparently minor elements. Sometimes a little phrase becomes crucial, and secondary roles may have a major function. One must pay heed to this in performance and not, as in Italian opera, settle for third-rate singers in *comprimario* parts that no one even listens to!

C.S. Russian melody is, after all, the meeting point of the classical heritage and the folklore tradition.

G.V. Indeed, Russian composers rely on folklore as a foundation. They string together long phrases: in one spot you recognize a tune, in another the form of a folk song. But one should also take the individuality of the language into account.

C.S. Can great Italian or French singers sing in Russian and still do justice to the musical structure of the text?

G.V. One cannot force them to sing like Russians. If they have a remarkable voice, I'll put up with it. When the voice is bad, perfect Russian pronunciation isn't going to improve it. But I have a great deal of respect for the foreign singers who learn a role in Russian, for it's a colossal task.

C.S. Have you yourself often sung in other languages?

G.V. As far as opera is concerned, I've sung only in Italian, and I think singing in Italian is easier on the voice than singing in Russian. The Italian language is made for singing, and the roles I've performed in both languages have posed fewer problems for me in Italian than in Russian.

C.S. What about French—

G.V. I have sung Landowski in French. French is difficult for me, for the voice is placed differently. The vocal placement is closely tied to the spoken language; hence the importance of the mother tongue in a singer's training. As an experiment, I'd like to teach an Oriental child not his own language, but Italian for example—and see how it turns out. Because the voice doesn't depend only on the morphological makeup of the throat; it's subject to the operation of the muscles that control the emission of sounds. I actually have a particular singer in mind, quite the classic Oriental type, but who has studied at the Moscow Conservatory. He's a remarkable Boris with slanted eyes, his voice perfectly adapted to the music of Mussorgsky, but he has always lived in Europe.

C.S. Let's talk about Mussorgsky. Very Russian but not necessarily very accessible to the Russian public—

G.V. Yes, in Russia the general public still thinks *Khovanshchina* is a difficult opera.

C.S. In the case of *Boris Godunov*, a national symbol, its format is far from standardized, if only because of the different versions in use. Being the conductor you are, Slava, you must have an opinion about this.

M.R. I have sworn to myself to conduct, at least once in my life, each of the versions of *Boris*: Rimsky-Korsakov's (the most popular), Shostakovich's, and then the original version.

C.S. Both original versions—

M.R. The one edited by Paul Lamm and the other one, which is by Mussorgsky only, with no outside additions.

C.S. When an original score exists, does one have the right to make changes?

M.R. Yes, and I'll tell you why. There is, on the one hand, something I'll call "elementary musical education" and, on the other, genius. Now Mussorgsky, at least as far as I know, practically never heard his works in their orchestrated form. He had some brilliant ideas, but quite often his ideas don't sound in the orchestra. This is what Shostakovich used to say to me, and he himself would not have spent so much time orchestrating Mussorgsky's opera if it weren't for the immense admiration he had for him. He knew him better than anyone. He would tell me, "I'm doing everything Mussorgsky did. I am carrying out all his orchestral ideas." Now, without changing Mussorgsky's ideas, Shostakovich simply made them sound better in the orchestra, thanks to his technique for orchestration; he gave Mussorgsky's ideas a satisfying realization in sound.

I also think that as great a composer as Schumann made mistakes, mistakes that must be corrected. It is not always easy to redo an orchestration, so mistakes are tolerated while trying to disguise them as much as possible in performance.

C.S. But Rimsky-Korsakov went further: he "corrected" certain original chords, certain bold strokes which shocked him.

M.R. That's precisely what annoyed Shostakovich, and Shostakovich preserved all Mussorgsky's harmonies.

C.S. Nevertheless, isn't it dangerous to implement this sort of "touch-up job"? How is one to know if it's right—or if a masterpiece is being involuntarily mutilated?

M.R. I've spoken at length with Maurice Le Roux about this problem and do not agree with the thesis that he puts forth in his book on *Boris Godunov*. In any case, one cannot be categorical. Certain things can be felt only by intuition.

Personally, all through my life, I've been in contact with composers. While playing or conducting a score, I sometimes would think I had discovered a better solution and would tell the composer, who would strike his brow saying, "I wasn't satisfied with that passage, but I didn't know how to change it."

I simply mean to say that a composer may make a mistake on a specific point and come up with, for example, an idea that doesn't sound properly. I've known so many such cases! And that can happen to great composers who don't totally master the process of orchestration. I am certain that Mussorgsky was one of those.

C.S. But you concede that Mussorgsky is the most inventive of the Russian composers? The greatest genius? For the world as a whole, however, the most famous is Tchaikovsky.

M.R. For the Russians, too!

C.S. Yes, but the "experts" in the West sometimes look askance—

G.V. With Tchaikovsky it all depends on the interpretation. Too often, his music is made to sound effete. I myself have experimented with it. Early in my career, I devoted an entire recital to Tchaikovsky, and the audience had the impression they were hearing Tchaikovsky for the first time. Everything was different: the tempos, the colors. For example, that song entitled "Amid the Din of the Ball [*Sred shumnova bala*]," which everyone in Russia knows: I sang it differently and the public was surprised and then began to roar so vociferously that I had to sing it again. It was really an altogether different reading of the score.

M.R. The tragic thing about Tchaikovsky is that performers and music lovers all agree in thinking that his music is so facile, so totally accessible, and so popular that it's useless to read anything into it. I struggle with all my power against this false notion because I know a countless number of atrocious interpretations of *Swan Lake.* I believe, on the contrary, that one must think a great deal about Tchaikovsky's music and closely scrutinize the score before performing it. In our country, Tchaikovsky's music falls within a tradition, but that tradition is only the overabuse of elements of dubious taste preserved through several generations, whose only goal is to make a big effect. I'm thinking of the fermatas on high notes in the operas and of the tempos that past choreographers have imposed upon his ballets.

C.S. So Tchaikovsky's music is badly played?

M.R. Yes.

C.S. Even in Russia?

M.R. Yes.

C.S. Less so in Russia?

M.R. Less badly there, perhaps, but badly nonetheless.

C.S. Doesn't the character of Tchaikovsky bother you a little?

M.R. No, he's very close to my heart, and I'll tell you why. Tchaikovsky *is* Russia. It is not Mussorgsky's Russia, but the Russia of Tchaikovsky is close to me even though I bow more deeply before Mussorgsky. Tchaikovsky is St. Petersburg, he's the West, he's Europe. And the works of Tchaikovsky are closely tied to those of our greatest poet, Pushkin. Knowing Russia and Pushkin, knowing the harmony that exists between words, music, and nature, a Russian cannot fail to love Tchaikovsky. It's impossible. Whatever one may say, even if I were told he was a swindler or a thief. So he was homosexual? That was his affair.

C.S. Does the sentimentality of his music correspond to a deep lyricism in the Russian nature?

M.R. Yes, that's an interesting point. I think there's a certain discrepancy between Tchaikovsky's music and his private life. Everyone thinks his music is sentimental and that his life was that of a weak man, but I believe exactly the opposite. I don't believe his music is sentimental; it all depends on interpretation. His music is made out to be vapid, effeminate, though he's one of the most powerful of composers. And he doesn't need *me* to defend him. Stravinsky used to tell me, "Tchaikovsky is one of the greatest composers." Britten agreed, and Prokofiev too. Only Shostakovich said, "He's one of the worst!"

C.S. And was Stravinsky really Russian?

M.R. Yes, Stravinsky knew how to evoke his recollection of Russia, which for us remained totally true, like a picture in one's mind. Stravinsky handed down to us a striking portrait of Russia. Along with those of Prokofiev and Mussorgsky, his is the most authentic of Russias; Tchaikovsky comes next, if it's possible to establish this sort of hierarchy. For example, the prints you see over there on the wall are from *Petrushka*; they're representations of a period. There are the holidays, Mardi Gras, the Dance of the Coachmen, the popular gatherings. Likewise for *Les Noces*. Stravinsky's works are totally Russian, except perhaps those of the last period.

C.S. And what do you say about Stravinsky's neoclassic output? Are *Oedipus Rex, Symphony in Three Movements,* and *Jeu de cartes* still Russian?

M.R. Yes.

C.S. And even *The Rake's Progress?*

M.R. Yes, that's still Russian. For me, it starts being no longer Russian when he does his complicated contrapuntal pieces, ignores his heart, and begins to compose in the style of a computer in order to bring off an eleven-part fugue successfully. An eleven-part fugue is very difficult to write in a Russian style!

C.S. Galina, have you sung the music of Stravinsky?

G.V. Yes, in the early 1960s I performed his *Russian Songs* and excerpts from *Mavra*. At that time, Stravinsky was rarely played in Russia; his works were virtually banned, even though he was known to be one of the most Russian of composers. He always remained Russian, and I wonder if that faithfulness didn't bother him to a certain extent. He tried to fight his Russian nature—but without success, for it is impossible for a composer to renounce his inner temperament while maintaining the same level of quality for himself. Physically, Stravinsky reminded me of a character in a

Russian fairy tale: hand him a knotty wooden cane and he would look as if he had just emerged from a hollow tree in the forest. But, to return to his music, I feel the most Russian-sounding ones are, after all, those of his first period.

C.S. With Prokofiev, one cannot really speak of stylistic "periods."

M.R. No. In Prokofiev, there is obviously no parallel to Stravinsky's third period.

C.S. Since you knew Prokofiev well, could you explain why, after having chosen to emigrate after the Revolution of 1917, he went back to his native country in the 1930s to settle there permanently?

M.R. If Galina and I were to go to Russia now and give concerts, it would be dangerous for us. I'm not speaking of political risk. It would be dangerous because of the love the Soviet people might show us. Then it would be difficult to leave again. When I gave my last concert, on 10 May 1974, the people in the audience were crying and calling out to me, "Come back, promise you'll come back!" After the concert, they were waiting for me in the street— Now, Prokofiev went back several times to give concerts in Russia without deciding to remain permanently. He told me that he used to be welcomed with extraordinary enthusiasm; even people who didn't know his music celebrated him, even when he played out in the sticks. And even if nobody applauded him, they'd still hug and kiss him. Whether his music pleased or not, he was king; he knew it, and returned to Russia.

G.V. They soon stopped hugging and kissing him!

C.S. But why did they embrace him?

M.R. It's very simple. He came from abroad, where everything is better than home, as everyone knows! And he'd come back to see us; he'd come back to play at home! He was a famous genius.

G.V. He was a famous genius because it had been thus decided outside of Russia. At home, it is very important to be recognized abroad.

M.R. I won't mention the name of a very famous foreign cellist who was playing in Moscow. I attended the concert and was sitting alongside an excellent violinist, very direct and spontaneous, who recently died. The pianist sounded the A, and the cellist began to tune. And the violinist exclaimed, "What a musician!" without having heard a note of the score!

G.V. The guy sitting behind me added, "And now we know who the top cellist in the world is!"

C.S. Prokofiev left France, where he had had a few problems. But did he regret it in the end?

G.V. He did have some problems in France, but financial ones.

M.R. Later on, he missed Paris very much. He told me so.

C.S. When Russians emigrate, they seem to bring with them a whole national tradition. They surround themselves with Russian friends and speak Russian together. You two, for example, have redecorated your Parisian apartment in Russian style. Why?

G.V. Because we like it, and because it's beautiful. Not out of homesickness. It's the sort of atmosphere I grew up in. The treasures from Russian museums and the paintings are a part of my life. Even the ordinary items mean something to me. You see that wooden object on that table over there? You might prefer a collector's item to it, but to me it's really very pretty. That's the kind of beauty we cannot do without; it's not merely a nostalgic souvenir. And as for the language, the Russian language is my language, my culture.

M.R. To me, all these objects and furnishings have the look and feel of "Russian hands." The hands that made them have great significance. And with them we create the atmosphere of our home.

G.V. It's also a way of evoking the history of our country. Look at Russian porcelain: one can trace in it the labor of the serfs, one can marvel at how, by the crude light of a torch, they were able to produce such intricate designs. This is all the history of my country; it's my life.

M.R. For my part, I must say that my inner life and imagination are much more important than real life and these objects around me. I have all of Russia in my mind and never detach myself from it. I am very proud to consider myself an ambassador of Russia. If Russia were led by an intelligent man, he would have decorated us with the greatest of honors, because we bring the music of Russia to other lands and assume the responsibility wholeheartedly. I, for one, am aware of the great honor this represents. As a matter of fact, I still have a great many plans in this area: making recordings of all the symphonies of Prokofiev and Shostakovich. I still dream of recording a few Russian operas. Yes, I have a lot of work in mind. I must say that the Soviet recording of *Katerina Izmaylova* is very bad, and I wonder when they will be able to produce a recording to compare with the one we made. In Moscow, even technology lies!

C.S. Generations pass, and so do memories. How do you think your daughters, who were still so young when they left Russia, will live and pass on your national heritage?

M.R. The ties will get weaker. They're already slackening more and more. You notice it in the older defectors: their children speak less Russian, and most of the time the grand-children no longer speak it at all!

C.S. Your dream—

M.R. Our dream remains Russia, where, in happier days, we could have lived.

Same couple, same repertoire, same artistic complicity— twenty years apart: left, in 1960, and below, celebrating their twenty-fifth wedding anniversary in Paris, 1980. Photos A.P.N.; Bulka, Gamma.

Rostropovich and Khrushchev. What is hidden behind the official smiles? Photo Raskin, Magnum.

The Rostropovich *dacha* in Zhukovka where Solzhenitsyn stayed in 1969, thus setting in motion the irreversible course of controversial political events. Photo Steiner, Stern.

Rostropovich and Galina Vishnevskaya paid stirring homage to their friend Sakharov in the Salle Pleyel, 27 February 1980. Twenty-four cellists responded to Slava's invitation; the music of Villa-Lobos capped off the unforgettable evening. Photo Lochon, Apesteguy, Gamma.

Galina and Slava held an emotional press conference in Paris on 15 March 1978, after hearing on a television newscast that the Soviet government had revoked their citizenship. Photo Simonet, Gamma.

Pablo Casals, or the first cellist *assoluto*. Photo CBS.

Benjamin Britten, inspired by Galina's voice and Slava's bow. Photo Clive Barda.

ostropovich enjoying a moment with Leonard Bernstein. According to *Time* magazine, Slava the man of five Fs: Fiddles, Food, Females, Friends, and Fodka. Photo G. Neuvecelle.

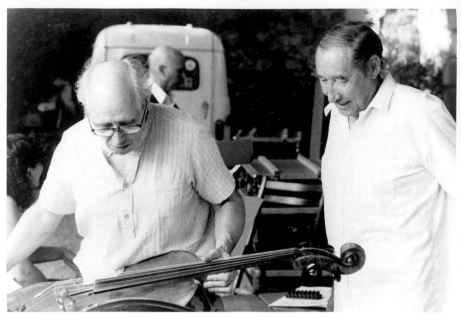

Rostropovich consults with luthier Etienne Vatelot, "the doctor of our instruments."
Photo Roger Picard, Radio France.

Slava with fellow activists in the contemporary music scene, Henri Dutilleux (right) and
Witold Lutoslawski. Photo G. Neuvecelle.

...ava, intent and inspired.
...oto Roger Picard,
...dio France.

Professorial.
Photo Cormier.

Tender and lyrical.
Photo G. Neuvecelle.

Rostropovich under Karajan's baton, a prestigious pairing repeated for many concerts and historic recordings. Photo S. Lauterwasser.

The diva in her signature role: Tatiana in *Eugene Onegin*. Galina grew up with the Pushkin character as set to music by Tchaikovsky, triumphed in the part at the Bolshoi, and chose it for her farewell performances at the Paris Opéra in 1982. Photo Roger Picard.

Younger daughter Elena, the pianist, here taking a bow with her parents at the Festival de Gourdon, July 1976. Photo Artault, Gamma.

Olga, the elder daughter and a cellist, accompanied her parents on their historic return to Russia in February of 1990. Photo A.F.P.

Rostropovich and Claude Samuel in conversation, 29 November 1989. Photo Roger Picard, Radio France.

At the Théatre des Champs-Elysées, Slava as soloist with the Orchestre National de France under the direction of Yan Pascal Tortelier, 9 December 1991. Photos Roger Picard, Radio France.

Rostropovich was director of his "musical family," the National Symphony
Orchestra, from 1977 to 1994. At the end of a farewell season that included a ten-day
tour of Russia and the Baltics, the baton passed to Leonard Slatkin. Photos courtesy
National Symphony Orchestra.

A formal portrait, Slava with the National Symphony in the Concert Hall of the John F. Kennedy Center for the Performing Arts, 1992. Photo courtesy National Symphony Orchestra.

26 September 1993: Rostropovich and the National Symphony perform a free concert in Moscow's Red Square for an enthusiastic crowd, Boris Yeltsin among them, even as opposing hard-liners remained closeted in Parliament. Photo Zemlianichenko, AP/Wide World Photos.

Music Under the One-Party Regime

C.S. Music lovers often think of musicians as people who live in an ivory tower. In the service of so-called eternal musical values, the performer doesn't have to worry about the way the world is run or about the drudgery of everyday life. In any case, politics plays no part in a performer's agenda. Music is a privileged domain. Or is it?

M.R. I'd like to sum up what I've been doing these past few days. Yesterday, in Rome, I conducted the same program for the third time, and the musicians of the orchestra played even better than they had the first two days. It was perhaps the best they had ever played in their lives! I don't claim this to be the result of my conducting ability; they simply loved me more as a human being, and my love for them had also increased. Afterward, we drank some champagne, a few musicians came with me to a restaurant that was still open (to my misfortune, perhaps), and we ended up staying there until three o'clock in the morning.

That is an absolutely indispensable part of my activity. Especially after a concert has gone well, it is necessary to prolong the success with human contact.

But to get back to what I started to say: the artist is obliged to love the people for whom and with whom he plays. For me, that's something obvious; without it, the artist's activity becomes a cross to be borne continually.

If you like people, you must be honest with them. If your friends are in a difficult situation or in danger, how could you remain silent? Galina and I have decades of experience behind us, so how could we hide what our own experience has taught us perfectly well? It would be dishonest.

I recently spent a few hours in Paris, *en route* from Rome to New York. But Galina and I took the time there to join a protest in support of Sakharov, outside of the Soviet embassy. Beyond the political issue, Sakharov is simply our personal friend; he lived opposite us in the country, and we used to see him quite often. I'll never forget the time Shostakovich was forced, really forced, to sign a letter against Sakharov. Shostakovich tried to explain why he didn't want to sign: "I'm very weak,"—and he really was ill at the time—"the only place where I can still take a stroll is around my country house. Unfortunately, that's where Sakharov sometimes walks. How could I look him in the eye if my signature is put at the bottom of this letter?" He was forced to sign, however. He really agonized over it, and he stopped taking walks.

C.S. Would you have signed that letter if pressured?

M.R. No. Absolutely not. Galina and I have refused to sign a number of letters, even very brief letters.

C.S. So Shostakovich could have refused?

M.R. I don't blame him. He was very ill with cancer.

I have another memory on this subject. It was during the days when they had stopped inviting me to the Bolshoi. One day, I went all the same to hear *Eugene Onegin* under the direction of another conductor; I was really horrified at the interpretation, and Galina knows how much I suffered. That's when two artists from the Bolshoi came to me to ask me to sign a letter against Sakharov. If I signed it, I would be able to go back and conduct at the Bolshoi the next day. It's obvious that the letter remained unsigned, not only because I refused, but also because I have a wife who would never have accepted either.

But I'd like to go back to the comment Roland Leroy recently made about me during a radio program. He said: "I don't agree with the political opinions of Rostropovich. He's a brilliant musician, but not a brilliant politician." I answered him by saying I agreed. It's very difficult to separate politics from life, but there are nevertheless some human qualities which must be considered outside of any political context.

Take Poland: the situation is very serious, the Poles have nothing to eat and are on the brink of civil war. Let's not speak of the reasons behind it; forget the political point of view. But Galina and I have friends in Poland: Lutoslawski, Penderecki, hundreds of people we love. Can we remain indifferent? No. We don't have the right to.

That's why the day before yesterday in Rome, one hour before my concert, already in formal evening dress, I joined a crowd that had assembled in St. Peter's Square. I prayed with the crowd for Poland. It's my artistic duty. It makes no difference what country: wherever people are suffering, our help is needed. And wherever we can do something, even if it's only to pray, it must be done.

G.V. Yes, but it's easy to say that, because we are living here, in a free country. When you live in Russia, what can you do? How can Soviet artists be accused of not supporting Poland?

If they make one move, they'll be arrested, just like that.

One can indeed speak of the artist in terms of isolation. In Russia, we were completely isolated from the rest of society. My life was spent between home and the Bolshoi. That was all. I didn't want to know about anything else, for it was the only way to survive in that country. I would go back home and shut the door; it was my domain, and I wouldn't let anyone in. I had very few friends, probably because I attach great importance to friendship. My husband says he has lots of friends, but he doesn't really: he has innumerable acquaintances. Naturally, I have many acquaintances too, but true friends— I've always had very few of those. When I say "true friends," that means people to whom I can speak openly and in whom I have total confidence. In Russia, I had no such friends.

What's more, over there you were always afraid "friends" would betray you sooner or later. In a system where the government pushes people to act underhandedly, to build a career on dirty tricks, and to obtain personal benefits by being an informant, how can you help fearing that a friend might betray you for material gain?

Here, we are free and don't have the right to take refuge in silence. It wouldn't be the right thing to do. Liberated from the constraints of Soviet society, if something annoys me, I must express myself. How could I dare be silent here? If an artist chooses isolation, that attitude doesn't have the same meaning as in Russia or in another totalitarian state. Here, it would be considered indifference and not be tolerated. An artist whose ambition is to express emotions cannot by nature be apathetic. And I would doubt the integrity of an artist who reserved his emotions for the stage while remaining insensitive to the injustices of life.

C.S. So, for the Soviet artist, the choice is between silence and defection?

G.V. Yes, that's what we did. We would stay home and live only for our art. Then the moment of our encounter with Solzhenitsyn arrived, and we entered into open opposition against the regime, against the lie. You know how that turned out! We found ourselves back here, which is to say we were chased out!

M.R. What Galina says is quite right, though I'd like to add something about friends and acquaintances. In Moscow, after a performance, Galina was always surrounded by flocks of admirers whom we'd receive at home. Friends, or acquaintances? It made little difference! I'll add only one thing. Imagine yourself in the company of someone whom you consider your friend. And, in the friendliest of manners, he says to you, "You know, life is atrocious in this country! What corruption!" And you start thinking, "He might be an undercover agent—" In Russia, this has become a sickness. So, whenever you speak sincerely to a friend, even a very close friend, you instantly feel you are being shut out.

For example, let's take Shostakovich or Prokofiev. Obviously they could not be accused or even suspected of being agents. Yet, sometimes, if someone else had said the same sorts of things to me as Shostakovich or Prokofiev said, well, I would have been afraid and stopped the conversation. Because that type of provocation is rampant at home. They send us people who are violently critical of the regime to make us respond in the same way.

G.V. And that's how those people win the confidence of the Soviet government, which is to say the confidence of the superpowers of this world. Thus they obtain important benefits and get ahead in their careers more easily.

C.S. Prokofiev is an interesting case because he lived in Russia before it became Soviet and he knew Western Europe before returning voluntarily to the Soviet Union. Back in Russia, it appears he remained silent, and, to judge from works like *War and Peace*, it seems even he sometimes bowed to the canons of the regime.

M.R. I'd like to point out a few basic truths. First of all, when Prokofiev came back to Russia, he could no longer leave the country—he couldn't go anywhere. If he had taken a long journey, he would only have ended up in Siberia. It was clear to everyone, and to him especially: he was caught in a mousetrap.

Next, Prokofiev was highly egotistical and only interested in his work. He knew that his composing career would be more brilliant in his native land than abroad. Of that he was convinced.

Finally, the most important element: what could he do? He would often say to me, "I don't want to die until I hear *War and Peace* again." He was referring to the definitive version of his opera, but nevertheless he died without having heard it. And he never heard a performance of his *Sinfonia Concertante* in its new form.

In the Soviet Union, fulfilling even the most legitimate desires is strangely problematical, and when you outsiders ask us questions, you must realize that Russia is a different world entirely. Here in Paris, no one can understand, no one will ever understand. After having lived in the West for eight years, we too have changed. Before, we would never speak so frankly, even to each other.

G.V. For the first time, we are beginning to live. In Russia, as I told you, we lived only for our art. I had my opera house, Slava had his cello and his Conservatory, which is to say a profession, a job. That's where we communicated our feelings; that's where we could be sincere. With his cello, Slava expresses anything he wants, and it was a great consolation to him then. As for me, in ordinary life I was very withdrawn, much more so than Slava—but on the stage, what a turnabout!

Today, we're living real lives. Over there, our life was the theater. Everything was backwards. We were actors in life and human beings on the stage.

M.R. It's difficult to imagine the extent to which the brain degenerates when one is living under the Soviet regime. I'll take the Supreme Soviet elections as an example. First, for several weeks, departmental delegates verify the electoral residency lists. The day of the election, starting at seven in the morning, music is piped into the streets and flags are everywhere. Propagandists come to your home and tell you to hurry up. They tell you all the details they know about the candidates' lives and, of course, run down the list of their medals. Each propagandist is responsible for his neighborhood, and his only concern is to get finished as soon as possible. So he doesn't hesitate to drag you out of bed at the crack of dawn. For Galina and me, getting up at eight o'clock was early enough. In any case, there was no question of going any later to vote, since we wouldn't be allowed to sleep.

Then, what was there to do? You're given the printed ballot bearing the name of *one single* candidate, and you have to put it in the ballot box! Not two candidates, only one! What is there to think about? "They" have already done your thinking for you! The candidate has already been chosen, you have only to drop his name in the ballot box and that's it. Next you go to a shop, wait in line to buy groceries, and waste two precious hours of your life. Really, what's to think about? Playing your instrument a little faster, having a drink, and going to sleep!

C.S. You who have experienced a totalitarian political system, the inner workings of which might vary but the cases of which are unfortunately innumerable, do you think that under such a system the artist has any role to play, or even a responsibility to assume? That, in any case, he is in a unique position in such a society?

M.R. A very interesting question. I won't try to cover the entire history of the world, but let me go back at least as far as the Renaissance. In Florence, the Medici appreciated art and commissioned works from favorite painters; their choices naturally reflected their own tastes. But there were also the Strozzi, who had different tastes and commissioned works according to their own preference. Art was able to develop in different directions because each patron cultivated his own taste and particular culture, and artists could apply to different protectors.

In a totalitarian regime, there is only one "protector," the government. Everyone must answer to the government. Differences no longer exist since every new creation must toe the party line.

Today in Paris we appreciate the importance of IRCAM, directed by Pierre Boulez. I like Pierre very much; he is an absolutely brilliant musician, but going by what I hear, he defends his own line because it reflects his personal preferences. But at the same time, at the Théâtre des Champs-Elysées, the Salle Pleyel or elsewhere, other musicians can present works totally antithetical to Boulez's taste. In the Soviet Union, just try to go against the taste of Mr. Khrennikov: the whole Soviet Union will close the door on you. That's the totalitarian system: there is one single dictator. He polices the musical highways and makes sure all the cars travel in the same direction. And if he sees one going the wrong way, he immediately sets up a roadblock.

C.S. In the days of the czars, an artist also had to conform to the demands of those in power.

G.V. It wasn't the same thing at all! Then too there were numerous patrons with differing tastes. The imperial theater had its own political makeup, doubtless reflecting the tastes of the court or the czar, but other theaters could follow their own paths.

M.R. The most varied of aesthetic movements could develop; artists frequented whichever group or circle they liked. Thus, at the turn of the century, a painters' movement called the *Exposition ambulante* [Traveling Exhibition] came about. In their paintings, the artists in this group often depicted the poverty of the people, a theme obviously not dictated to them by the czar; nevertheless, it existed, for the most diverse of artistic trends could be expressed. Remember, too, that Prokofiev composed his first works before the Revolution, during the reign of Rimsky-Korsakov and Glazunov. In 1914, after completing his studies at the Conservatory, Prokofiev played his First Piano Concerto, and the performance provoked a great scandal. Glazunov, who was the director of the Conservatory, left the concert hall in indignation, though nobody forbade Prokofiev to compose that type of music.

C.S. Aren't relationships between the ruling class and the artist always rather ambiguous? And, whether the social structure is aristocratic or liberal, under the Medici for example, isn't the freedom of the artist the alibi or good conscience of the ruling class?

G.V. The Medici didn't look upon artistic creativity as an alibi; they acted out of love for art, not to pass on a flattering image of themselves to their descendants. For them, protecting artists stemmed from a personal need and reflected a love for works of art.

C.S. Even so, the artists had to obey! Archbishop Colloredo's restrictions on Mozart in Salzburg are well known—

M.R. But Mozart was able to leave Salzburg and settle in Vienna—

C.S. —to die of starvation there—

M.R. I agree, but can the Archbishop of Salzburg be compared with the whole Soviet government rolled into one?

G.V. The Archbishop of Salzburg paid for what he wanted and not for what he didn't want—but at least he didn't throw Mozart in prison! Mozart was free to compose the music of his choice and to perform it in public. In Russia, you not only have no right to compose music that comes from your heart, but chances are no one would perform it. No orchestra would dare play it. Your home would be stacked with tons of scores that you'd never hear a note of; you'd never have the experience of a live performance.

M.R. Soviet composers have two sources of income, one of which is the state commission, the only authorized type of commission. No individual has the right to commission works, which would be considered exploitation of man by his fellow man. Only the government has that privilege. To start, they advance a certain amount of money; then, when the composer presents the half-finished work, they grant a second advance—and finally, when the score is completed, they settle the balance. Later on—and this is one's second source of income—the composer receives royalties as performances occur. But if the composer doesn't follow the official line, he immediately loses both sources of income and all hope of future commissions; his only recourse is to search for a job in another line of work. As far as the government is concerned, he's blacklisted! Thus rejected, a composer cannot get his music played anywhere, because the censor is ever watchful.

Therefore, everyone depends on the central power, which

is to say a one-party taste that allows only very slight departures from the norm. There are some rare exceptions: Denisov, for example. Denisov earned his living by teaching music theory at the Conservatory, but there was no question of his earning any income as a composer. Then, little by little, his music started getting played abroad, which ultimately lent his music an aura of scandal in Russia. It's the same with Schnittke: he encountered great difficulties trying to get his music played until the day conductor Gennadi Rozhdestvensky gave him a break in Gorki, the town sadly famous today as the site of the forced internal exile of Sakharov. Schnittke's was the only sold-out concert, and people came from as far away as Moscow to attend it; many young people who were unable to pay for a train ticket grabbed onto the sides of the cars and rode standing on the running boards!

At the beginning of the symphony, a trumpet player runs onto the stage and starts playing like a madman. What happened in the Gorki concert hall? Nothing, because the Communist president of the region, who wasn't expecting such a bombshell, was fast asleep at that crucial moment. But later performances of Schnittke's piece suffered repercussions, and certain musicians were reprimanded. A real revolution—which helped Schnittke become known. Of course, a second hearing was out of the question. You see, with a little luck, one can sometimes slip through the mousetrap. But never in Moscow! And never in Leningrad!

C.S. But this repression that you are denouncing, and which today is the rule, was not always enforced in the Soviet Union. After the October Revolution, the avant-garde established itself in public circles, the oft-cited symbolic example being *Wozzeck*, performed in Leningrad in 1929!

M.R. Yes, the Revolution at first gave rise to a great feeling of hope. Luigi Nono* championed that point of view before

*Italian composer born in 1924, whose Communist sympathies are known.

Khrennikov. He told him, "You claim to be a revolutionary force; you think you're at the forefront of every domain. Then, why do you oblige your composers to write conservative music?" Luigi Nono was right. In 1917, the revolutionaries felt they were on the way to freedom, and a very rich artistic movement began to develop. There was Meyerhold, a revolutionary and a brilliant actor/director. They say he used to walk around in a leather jacket with a revolver, but he staged productions which have become part of theatrical history. And, because he was a genius, he died in a concentration camp. As for Kandinsky, for two years he headed the Painters' Union, but he left Russia in 1921. What would have happened if he hadn't escaped? He too would have been sent to die in a gulag, for he couldn't change his way of painting. Or he would have had to paint portraits of Lenin, Stalin, Brezhnev, and company!

C.S. Although nothing can justify its inhumanity, of course, cannot this situation be explained by the fact that, in the early years of Communism, the revolutionaries, who sincerely wished to place art on a level with the people, quickly saw that the experimental art of the time, at odds with tradition and sometimes hard to understand, was unavoidably divorced from the people for which it was intended? And therefore it was with all good intentions that the revolutionaries swung in the direction that led to the establishment of a peculiar type of artistic dictatorship.

M.R. Yes, that's very interesting! I would have understood perfectly if in 1948 Jdanov had assembled the composers all together and said, "We respectfully salute Prokofiev and Shostakovich and feel they represent the avant-garde of Soviet music; but the people are not ready for this avant-garde. So we must give them what they want: after all, some like fish while others prefer beef. To the people, therefore, we shall give songs or accessible symphonic works. Dear composers, take care of this need, for we know that a large portion of our population does not appreciate classical music. But we are not ignorant of the value of classical music, we warmly salute the Prokofievs and the Shostakoviches, and we will not prevent them from experimenting."

Had it been expressed thus, I would have understood the politicians' concern for trying to make artistic values more accessible to the public. But on the contrary, they turned to the first collective farmer and asked for his opinion:

"Tell us, do you like the music of Shostakovich?"

"I don't know a thing about music!"

"Well, that's precisely why we asked you for your opinion."

And the opinions of all the collective farmers were faithfully reported in the newspapers. Personally, I know of no composer of genius in the history of music whose works were immediately accepted by the public. Sometimes a great composer may gain wide recognition toward the end of his life, but at the beginning of his career he is supported by only a small group of admirers, which is completely understandable. Can one reverse the course of history the better to conform to Jdanov's orders? "You know Tchaikovsky, don't you? Good—then write like him!"

G.V. Indeed, according to Jdanov, the same music had to be heard by everyone, from the peasant and factory worker to the Ph.D. But we know this is impossible. There are peasants, and also intellectuals, who can do without the symphonies of Beethoven or Tchaikovsky. At any rate, the government feels that it alone is capable of expressing the wishes of the people. It's not enough for the government to force this simplistic reasoning on the peasants and factory workers, it forces it on the intelligentsia, too. Quite simply because the government officials know nothing about music. They never hear any and certainly have no need for it.

M.R. Imagine. Tomorrow, François Mitterand attends a concert of works by Pierre Boulez, and the next day the music of Pierre Boulez is banned all over France. Could this happen?

C.S. I cannot conceive of its happening—

M.R. But that's exactly what has occurred back home, and more than once! The misfortune happened twice to Shostakovich. One single man banned everything.

I'd like to share an anecdote. A rather important government official had just died, and a funeral ceremony was taking place in the large Hall of Columns in the House of the Unions—a ceremony accompanied by the best Soviet chamber ensemble of the day, the Beethoven Quartet, founded some fifty years before. I was waiting to rehearse with those very members of the Quartet when I saw the first violinist enter, trembling.

"No, I cannot play anymore, I simply cannot!"

"What happened?"

"We were just beginning to play when Stalin positioned himself at attention in front of the casket, right next to us. My bow was shaking so much, I couldn't play. It was all I could do to keep from dropping my bow! You can imagine what would have happened if I had dropped it! Stalin would have inquired, 'Who are those musicians?' And they would have replied, 'The members of the Beethoven Quartet.' And he would have shouted, 'Send them away!' "

The poor musician never recovered his composure. But I assure you, if I had played in front of Stalin, my bow would have been shaking too!

C.S. But wasn't there, at least during the 1920s, a sincere effort by some Communist leaders to establish a line of communication between art and the people? In the 1930s, when Prokofiev returned to the Soviet Union, he wrote in *Izvestia*: "I would qualify the music needed here as 'lightly serious' or 'seriously light'; it is not easy to find words to describe it."

M.R. That's exactly what I was saying. A large segment of the Soviet population has no musical training whatsoever and needs to be given a very simple kind of music. I once traveled across the country in the company of an accordionist, playing in the *isbas,* the most modest country homes—my cello and an accordion. The most difficult music I was able to play for them was Tchaikovsky! I also played them a famous polonaise by Oginski. It was awful music, but how they loved it! I knew if I played a work that was a little more complicated, they would turn their backs on music for the rest of their lives.

I was really the first artist to perform for the public in these lost villages, and I knew my audiences needed me. The government would have been on the right track if only it had asked for music these people could appreciate.

G.V. After all, it's not an absolute must for everyone to want music; people have the right to live without making music or having the slightest thing to do with it. But in Russia, composers are supported by the public: the people work, and artists are paid with their money, so the bureaucrats figure they have the right to tell composers, "If you take the people's money, have the decency to write music on their level! If you get your money from the pockets of the people, it's only fitting for you to renounce your artistic freedom."

M.R. Yes, Khrennikov solves all problems in the name of the people. "The people don't need it" is the stock phrase; it's all we hear!

C.S. Haven't there been at least some Soviet leaders who were interested in music?

G.V. I don't know of any.

111

M.R. Nor I. But they say Lenin is supposed to have heard the *Appassionata* Sonata once or twice in his life.

G.V. Anyway, whether or not he listened to music is of no importance. His successors didn't have to prevent others from doing what they wanted.

M.R. I remember that one day at the Moscow Conservatory, early in my teaching career, there was a sudden moment of panic. It was while Stalin was still alive. Classes came to a halt, bells rang in the halls, and all the teachers and students were herded like sheep into the auditorium. A red cloth was draped over the table, and Alexander Simeonov, a clarinetist—a bad one, by the way—who was the Party secretary for the Conservatory section, stood up and declared, "Comrades! Today we recall the happiest day in the history of the Moscow Conservatory. Thirty years ago today, Comrade Stalin attended a concert in this very hall." It was, in fact, the most famous concert hall in Moscow, but Stalin had never returned to it.

I played the fool and said to the person next to me, "To me, it's a shameful anniversary: in thirty years our leader has never once come back!" "Hold your tongue, idiot!"—

So why the panic? Because the day had almost gone by unnoticed! No doubt someone whispered to the secretary-comrade at the last minute, "Hey! Today's the anniversary!"

So, the speeches began, some on behalf of the students, others on behalf of the entire teaching faculty; then the director of the Conservatory himself exclaimed, "Just think! Thirty years ago, he sat over there, in person, in this hall, Comrade Stalin!"

C.S. Surely nobody was taken in by it?

M.R. Oh yes! They were sincerely paying homage!

112

G.V. Why did the violinist's hand tremble? Because Stalin mattered more than God!

C.S. Was it fear or conviction?

M.R. Both.

G.V. Hypnosis!

M.R. Fear, the fear of thinking.

G.V. Let's face it: Stalin was Superman!

C.S. I'd like you to describe for me in detail the grievances that the Soviet government has leveled, or is still leveling, at composers. I have the feeling that these grievances, particularly as far as opera is concerned, are aimed more at the subjects chosen than at the musical styles used.

M.R. The subject of the libretto is naturally the primary element. Before writing an opera, which is to say before writing the musical score, a composer must propose a subject. If the subject is not approved, the composer can still write his opera, but it won't be performed. It will be a stillborn child, petrified for centuries, for as long as the Soviet government endures.

To help get past the censor, some composers include distractingly improbable commentaries with their opera project proposals. With Muradeli's *October,* an opera which included Lenin among the dramatis personae, the discussion thus centered around the following question: Would Lenin sing? The censors decided that it was a possibility, but that he shouldn't sing all the time. So Muradeli gave him a speaking part, though at one point Lenin, in a suave baritone voice, sings a sad, sentimental folk song. Copies of the work were distributed to the singers before the score was printed, and I couldn't resist tearing out a page of the piano score that Galina was given. I had the page framed and hung it on the wall of my house in New York. It's a masterpiece—a masterpiece of stupidity!

I'll add that the Soviet government, as far as I can recall, has never had any major disputes with performers. On the contrary, it has always supported good performers, who occupy at least as important a place in the social hierarchy as that of composers. For instance, David Oistrakh's position was surely not inferior to that of Shostakovich. Why is this? Because performers have the resources of their repertoire. They aren't punished, but they are intimidated with orders to drop Shostakovich here, Schnittke there. That doesn't deprive the performer of his means of earning a living. He can always replace Shostakovich with Bach and Schnittke with Tchaikovsky, and life goes on. This privileged situation of performers explains why today the level of our school of performing is ultimately far superior to that of our school of composition.

C.S. Yes, but if, for example, we compare your career with that of Shostakovich, we notice that Shostakovich the composer, despite the governmental warnings, did not break away from the Soviet regime, while you stepped over the line.

M.R. If Solzhenitsyn hadn't come to stay with us, I'm convinced that we would have continued to live over there, especially since we had reached the top rung of the ladder.

C.S. Yes, but you don't mean that it was Solzhenitsyn's presence which triggered your hostility toward the Soviet regime!

M.R. Absolutely. When Solzhenitsyn first came to stay with us, there was no thought of our becoming political. It was simply a humanitarian act. When they wanted to force us to drive him out, that's when the bomb exploded. People would tell me, "You know, he's anti-Soviet!" And I would reply, "Before stating whether he is anti- or pro-Soviet, tell me if he is or is not a human being. He has to live somewhere, and we cannot turn him away. Give him an apartment or even a room, and he will leave of his own accord."

We were inextricably caught up in what was a humanitarian situation, pure and simple, and that's how we were turned into political figures. They told us we were supporting Solzhenitsyn. Obviously, we were supporting him, but what else could we do? Everyone should have acted in the same way!

C.S. When did your ties with Solzhenitsyn begin?

G.V. At first, there was no particular relationship. We knew Solzhenitsyn only as the author of *One Day in the Life of Ivan Denisovich* and a few other stories. We knew he was starting to have difficulties, but the attacks being aimed at him were still sporadic, and he was still a member of the Writers' Union. That's when Slava met him after a concert he was giving in Riazan and offered to take him in. The reason is quite simple: at that time, Solzhenitsyn and his family, four people in all, were packed into two little rooms in Riazan, while we had at our disposal a large country house with a little guest house that was unoccupied. So Slava invited Solzhenitsyn to spend the winter in the guest house; he accepted, and that's how I made his acquaintance. But I must say that, though the initial contact was made, it was difficult to foster a close relationship with him. Solzhenitsyn was an individualistic, withdrawn man, able to live alone for long periods of time—and I understand him all the more since I have the same kind of personality. When I was in our big house in the country, and he was living in the guest house, several weeks could go by without my running into him. He wasn't the kind of man who would visit people for the pleasure of chatting with them. He was absorbed in his work. He went to bed very early and would write all day long.

C.S. Did you ever have a chance to talk politics with him?

G.V. Oh, no. As I told you, we hardly ever conversed. But we were familiar with his ideas, and reading *One Day in the Life of Ivan Denisovich* had made a tremendous impression on us. We knew he was a great writer who was lacking the basic comforts of life, so we were only too happy to help him out. Then, *The Cancer Ward* was published outside of Russia, and the big Soviet literary journal began its mudslinging campaign against it. One year after coming to stay with us, he was dismissed from the Writers' Union. All these events occurred while he was under our roof. Now, looking out your window at what goes on across the street is much different from living the same situation in your own home. Our eyes were opened. We became aware of the nature of the regime under which we were living, and things we had been trying not to notice became clear to us. No longer could we say, "We don't want to know anything."

C.S. Did the Soviet authorities call you in for questioning?

G.V. Yes, we were summoned, and an important military chief spoke very nicely to us: "I must tell you that there is an unregistered man in your home, which happens to be located in a governmental zone. The local zoning rules are the problem. It would be better to have him leave." We refused, saying that it had nothing to do with any official registration since it was our house, and we invited whomever we wanted there. Obviously, if we had responded in that manner during the Stalin era, we wouldn't be here to tell you about it, and Solzhenitsyn would have been swiftly eliminated. The man answered, with a charming smile, that in that case our house might have to be taken away from us. And we told him that they could just try. This little game went on for nearly five years.

C.S. What really added fuel to the fire was the open letter that Slava sent to the Soviet newspapers, which never published it.*

G.V. But the letter was published in Paris.

C.S. Galina, did you agree with this letter?

G.V. I agreed with its contents, but at first I advised Slava not to write it. He was convinced it was a positive act, but I knew what we were risking. I knew we would be persecuted. I told him in no uncertain terms everything that was going to come of it, predicted every step of our adventure, and added, "You understand what I have just told you? And you still want to write that letter? Yes? Well then, you know what's in store for us." And everything happened just as I said it would. Without delay, the vice-minister of culture launched into an interrogation of me:
"Why didn't you protest?"
"Because he has the right to do what he feels is necessary."
"So you knew all about it?"
"Yes, I knew all about it."
"And you didn't make a report?" And so forth. Even Madame Furtseva, the minister of culture, was indignant: "How could Slava have done this?"
The persecutions began. In the opera house, I was still able to sing, but my name had disappeared. In everyone's eyes, I

---

*In that open letter of 31 October 1970, rejected by four Soviet newspapers but a copy of which was immediately—via a mysterious channel—sent to Western newspapers, Rostropovich wrote: "Why do decisions about our literature and our art so often belong to people who are absolutely incompetent in these fields? . . . Each human being must have the right to think for himself and to express his opinion without fear."

was conveniently dead. And some jealous colleagues didn't hesitate to take advantage of the situation. There were five Bolshoi singers—Atlantov, Masurok, Obraztsova, and company—who went to the Party Central Committee when I was embarking on the recording of *Tosca* with Slava. "How can this 'political outlaw' be allowed to remain on the roster of the Bolshoi? We Communists demand that he be dropped!" These were petty, insignificant individuals, thirsty for vengeance—they weren't even involved in the *Tosca* project—whose hour had finally come. In the Soviet Union, there have been several periods when political denunciation flourished. Everyone remembers the terror of 1937, and although this little band belonged to the new generation, they definitely recalled the conversations of their elders and followed their example.

C.S. You were caught in the trap, without ever having made the decision to oppose the regime openly.

M.R. At first, as Galina said, it was manifestly not a political dispute. At times I even thought Solzhenitsyn was going too far and could have expressed his opinion with greater moderation. But when we witnessed the absolutely inhuman, beastly attitude of his adversaries, that's when we began, thanks to him, to understand the reality. One day, he drove off in his car to spend a few weeks in Rostov, but he came back two days later. All over his body he had enormous blisters filled with pus. I took him to a friend's clinic, and that doctor-friend told me, "Under his name, I cannot even examine his heartbeat with my stethoscope." So, we gave him a pseudonym!

What is one to think of a political system that stoops to such absurdities?

C.S. And that's the system which celebrated your talents by awarding you, on a number of occasions, the Lenin Prize or the Stalin Prize—

M.R. Those prizes were the supreme honor. Yes, to this day I still feel it was an honor.

G.V. Not because the prize carried the name of Lenin or Stalin, but because it was *the* prize, the greatest award given in the Soviet Union.

M.R. One should know who awarded these prizes. On the committee of the Lenin Prize, there were, after all, Shostakovich and other top-drawer personalities. For film and literature, political reasons obviously influenced the selection, but in music the prizes were given to musicians of quality. It was truly a festive event. Can one say that Oistrakh, Gilels, and Richter didn't deserve a Lenin Prize? Those are great artists, and I maintain that the awarding of the prize represented a genuine honor.

C.S. An honor you paid dearly for—

M.R. Yes, we experienced, in return, the trials of persecution. They began to cancel some of our concerts, to omit our names in the press. I have a few fabulous reminiscences about this. One day in Gorki—once again Gorki!—I was conducting some works by Tchaikovsky, and Galina was singing Tatiana's Letter Scene. The Gorki newspaper published a more-than-flattering review of the concert, a veritable hymn in praise of the performers; the article was a little masterpiece in which the music critic somehow managed to avoid any mention of Galina's name or mine. I hope to find that article again some day.

G.V. It took up one half of an entire page!

M.R. The reporter wrote: "The orchestra displayed its brilliant sonorities . . . the concert was a great success . . . the interpretation of Tatiana's Letter Scene particularly impressed the audience . . . 'she' expressively conveyed the emotions of the young girl." But our names were nowhere to be seen. It was forbidden!

G.V. Our projects abroad were also disrupted. For instance, Karajan, who had heard me in *Eugene Onegin* when the Bolshoi performed it in Berlin, asked me to sing the role of Marina in the recording of *Boris Godunov* that he was to conduct, and I accepted. Then, as soon as certain Soviet officials were informed, and without discussing it with me, they turned him down, saying that I wasn't singing that role at the Bolshoi and that it wasn't right for my voice. I was in London when Karajan's secretary read me the letter that our minister of culture had just sent. When I returned to Moscow, I brandished the letter at the ministry, pounded the table, and shouted, "I know what I can and cannot do, and this is *my* business!" In the end, I was able to do the recording with Karajan.

C.S. Were you keeping in touch with your friends abroad?

G.V. Yes, Yehudi Menuhin would often phone, and French composers gave us their sympathy. But above all it was Leonard Bernstein who helped us and accelerated the process of our departure. We had, by this time, applied to the government for permission to leave Russia for two years and were waiting for the response. I would speak about it on the telephone to all my friends and scream into the receiver that if we hadn't obtained the permission within two weeks, I'd start breaking things. I screamed because I knew we were being bugged.

That was when Senator Edward Kennedy, to whom Bernstein had previously spoken, came to Moscow to see

120

Brezhnev. We weren't aware of any such proceedings. We knew that Senator Kennedy was in Moscow, but we didn't know his visit might concern us. And, suddenly, Kennedy's secretary phoned us with good news, saying that after the senator's conversation with Brezhnev, the situation should be quickly resolved. Two weeks later we received the permission. Madame Furtseva was the one who summoned us to let us know that we had obtained permission to leave the country for two years on an artistic tour.

C.S. Why do you think the Soviet government finally accepted the notion of your departure?

G.V. To be honest, I cannot explain it. I cannot understand why they let us leave with our children. Was it out of stupidity? Or was there a kind person among those who made the decision? In any case, it should be added that while all this was going on, the Party Central Committee had requested a memorandum concerning us. Khrennikov drafted a report—which we knew about—in which he explained that Rostropovich had been a good cellist at one time, but that his talent had diminished considerably over the past few years and that he had established friendly ties with Solzhenitsyn in order to boost his prestige abroad. The memorandum added that as far as Rostropovich's conducting career was concerned, everyone scoffed at it, and that, if he went abroad, he would ultimately learn his true worth— I didn't even want to know what Khrennikov wrote about me!

C.S. Now that we've heard this long political process through to its end, I'd like to ask you a rather blunt question. Before the Solzhenitsyn incident, if you—who were among the privileged class—had had the right to express your opinion (let's even imagine free elections), would you have voted for or against the regime?

121

M.R. and G.V. Against the regime, obviously!

G.V. If there were free elections, 90 percent of all Russians would vote against the regime.

M.R. We knew of, or rather, we suspected the evils of the system, and we suffered from them. All the more because we had made numerous trips abroad.

We Russians have a very strong curiosity about the people around us. It's very important for us to know what kind of life our neighbors are leading. It's typically Russian—

G.V. Not typically Russian, but Soviet!

M.R. In Russia, they tell the story of how, one day, God asked little Johnny his greatest wish, and Johnny answered: "I wish my neighbor Peter's cow would croak!" The important thing is knowing how we live in relation to others.

C.S. Going beyond the particular path which circumstances led you to follow, I'd like to return to the notion of the artist's responsibility, for I'm not sure that you specifically answered the question.

G.V. Oh, but I did answer it! An artist living in a totalitarian country can do nothing, or—as you well know—he will be immediately arrested. Sakharov went on a hunger strike, but do we have the right to demand such heroism of everyone? On the other hand, an artist who lives in the free world cannot compromise. He has all the power, and therefore the obligation, to speak, to express his opinions, and to protest.

M.R. I have another question to pose. Sakharov went on a hunger strike because Lise, his future daughter-in-law, couldn't join her fiancé who had already defected to the West.

Now, nobody in the Soviet Union needed Lise. One more or one less Lise among 260 million inhabitants: of what importance could it be? Everybody can understand that—above all, Sakharov's two hundred academic colleagues, who were cultivated men and great scholars. But I would like to know who among them stood up to defend Sakharov, their colleague, who was on the brink of the abyss. Not that they would have spared their gold to erect a monument to his glory. But they never had occasion to spend it. No one stood up, though everyone knew that Sakharov was right. In the Soviet Union, everyone understands that.

G.V. When I was living in the Soviet Union, I already thought, and I think more than ever today, that the academicians and scholars should have assembled and marched down the street together shouting, "Enough of this tyranny!" They wouldn't have been shot!

C.S. Why didn't they do it?

G.V. Because they were afraid! They're afraid in different ways. One is afraid he won't be able to get permission for his next trip abroad, another is afraid he won't get his raise—

M.R. —and someone else has a son finishing his secondary schooling who would like to enter the university—

G.V. Yes, what do they fear? Petty things! Under the system, people have become so small-minded that all ethical behavior has been quelled. Their only concern is getting a better loaf of bread than their neighbor's, gaining access to a store that is closed to other people, and buying a piece of sausage there while the neighbor has to wait five hours in line for the same amount of sausage! That's how they live, and that's why they haven't denounced the injustice.

C.S. What a great victory for the Soviet regime: the intellectuals are reduced to silence!

M.R. It must be said that it was accomplished at the cost of tens of millions of human lives!

G.V. Millions of people who were physically exterminated and others whose spiritual existence was stifled.

M.R. And I can assure you that that silence is not about to be broken.

C.S. As for the silence of the composers—

M.R. The composers? Do you think my great friend Shostakovich who wrote some works especially for me, my close friend Khachaturian, or a composer like Kabalevsky didn't know what I was going through when I was being persecuted? They knew! Shostakovich and Khachaturian saw me weeping several times. Couldn't they all have gone together to see the members of the government, to tell them, "You know, Rostropovich is an artist who can still serve Soviet music; he can be of great musical use to us, so don't dismiss him! He has numerous students, and you're apt to weaken our cello program—"? None of them tried that approach because, if they had stepped forward, Brezhnev would have raised his eyebrow and, with one eye shut, would have murmured, "Yes, he might not be a bad musician, but he isn't on our side! How could you think of pleading his case? How could you make such a mistake?"

G.V. And, the following year, as a result of their behavior in the matter, one of them might not receive the Lenin Prize!

M.R. However strongly Galina and I describe the situation to you, we really feel it's difficult to explain it all to you in words. But when you live over there, when it's your skin on the line, it's a different matter!

G.V. Future generations will be appalled by the Soviet regime's misdeeds, but won't they be even more appalled at the silence of the free world? Here, anything is possible. Mouths, ears, and eyes are open, but the people don't want to understand what's happening over there. They don't *want* to. And that's an international refusal. You can scream all you want, they plug their ears. When you tell them, "Look, I'm bleeding, I'm being skinned alive!" they answer, "No, it isn't true!"

C.S. What can someone who is a Soviet dissident do in the West?

M.R. My duty is to explain what I know, honestly, everywhere, to tell what I myself have endured.

G.V. And if we don't use this opportunity, it's a crime against all those who remain over there.

M.R. If we had come to the West as Soviet artists on tour, we wouldn't have been able to say half of one word of what we are saying today. Because we would have left our children over there, and we know very well that half a word would have been enough: from the moment we returned to Russia, our lives would have been over. I understand all the Soviet artists who remain silent. If I were still a Soviet artist, I would be silent too. We all kept quiet.

C.S. Today, on the contrary, one of your ambitions is to put pressure on Western governments.

G.V. We tell the stories, we speak of everything that we endured, everything we know, and the people themselves must draw their own conclusions.

M.R. We're not trying to tell anyone what to do, whether they be our friends, or kings, or presidents.

G.V. But when people question us, we tell the truth.

C.S. Don't you think that the silence of the West might be justified by the necessity of peaceful world coexistence? Being silent—to live in peace?

G.V. That was already done under Hitler, and that was enough! The method has been tried. Now maybe we should try another approach: force or disobedience—

M.R. And, furthermore, if the West doesn't try to stop it, the Soviet Union will develop into a colossal power. It's obvious the Russians will use that power, otherwise why would it exist? The moment the Soviet Union realizes its military strength, it's ready to use it. And, under such circumstances, what's the sense of silence?

A Question of Confidence

C.S. Slava, do you recall the first concert you ever conducted?

M.R. I don't know exactly which concert I would call my first. In fact, I began my conducting career in a somewhat unusual way, by directing small groups or cello ensembles, but nevertheless what I *could* call my first concert in front of an orchestra is a concert I co-directed with Shostakovich—

G.V. Who was himself conducting for the first time in his life—

M.R. —and also the last.

G.V. Personally, I clearly recall that concert, which took place in Gorki in 1961. The second half of the program consisted of interludes from *Lady Macbeth of Mtsensk* and *Songs and Dances of Death* by Mussorgsky in the Shostakovich orchestration,

127

with me as soloist. It was an insane program. Can you imagine? Rostropovich's temperament allied with the music of Shostakovich! With his brilliant intuition coupled with his lack, at that time, of conducting technique, I thought Slava would fly into a thousand pieces. But in the end he achieved what he wanted. And we repeated the exact same program in Moscow a week later.

M.R. But Shostakovich no longer conducted.

C.S. Did you take any classes in conducting?

M.R. No! Never in my life! I should say that in that first concert, the presence of Shostakovich, who was as new to it as I, put me at ease.

G.V. You forgot to mention that you had gone to Gorki beforehand to prepare the orchestra for Shostakovich. On his half of the program were the *Festive Overture* and the First Cello Concerto, in which you were the soloist. And you had the orchestra rehearse so much that they truly played by heart!

C.S. When did you first feel the urge to conduct?

M.R. Conducting an orchestra was a dream of mine from the moment I first came in contact with music, well before I ever touched a cello. By the time I was six, a conductor had already shown me some scores and explained the concept of transposing instruments. If I hadn't been encouraged to study the cello, my first choice would surely have been conducting an orchestra.

C.S. You ultimately became a conductor without going through the usual pedagogical channels. Can a young musician conduct without taking conducting classes?

M.R. No. On the contrary, it's very important to study. In my case, countless pieces of advice were given to me. Karajan, for example, taught me a very special trick in Shostakovich's Fifth Symphony. For *Eugene Onegin,* I was greatly helped by the experience of a Bolshoi conductor named Boris Khaikin, and for the concert in which I conducted the Prokofiev Fifth Symphony and Tchaikovsky's First Suite, I followed Kondrashin's counsel.

Naturally, as a cellist, I've had the chance to meet the greatest conductors in the world, but I've also met with them specifically to ask for their help in solving certain problems related to conducting. That said, despite everything, the importance of baton technique is relative. Today, certain conductors have highly polished techniques and a whole range of very clear and elegant gestures at their command. But it's like people who have beautiful handwriting: the quality of the penmanship is less interesting than the meaning of the text written.

Alas, young conductors are too often unaware of this. They figure that their physical dexterity makes up for the deficiencies in their musical knowledge. In reality, these shortcomings already create a handicap in the relationship between the conductor and the orchestra members. The conductor must have the kind of education that places him on a level with the instrumentalists, but he must also possess that "something extra."

Certain conductors have only two ambitions: keep it clear, and keep it together. These, after all, are not such difficult goals to achieve. But the genuine interpretation of a work requires a loftier objective, which is musical comprehension. After the Revolution, the Soviets did an experiment: they created a musical ensemble called "Persimfans," which means "first symphonic ensemble." Persimfans played the most difficult programs, without a conductor. That way they could make everyone collectively responsible for all decisions. How did the operation turn out? Interesting on a purely experimental plane, but not convincing on a musical level. Indeed, who was building the music (I say "building the music" in the way one speaks of "building a house")? Nobody! The musicians tried to play together; all the bricks were individually placed, but the house still wasn't there. Once again, that proves the importance of the conductor's personality.

I haven't seen Fellini's film *La prova d'orchestra* [The Orchestra Rehearsal], but I know what it's about and think it's a very fair portrayal. No matter how much the orchestra hates its conductor, such antagonism is normal and inevitable. It's part of human nature. However, some individuals have a greater capacity than others for directing a collective group. But that capacity is necessarily accompanied by a high degree of technical skill. For example, the conductor must know the bowing positions and fingerings, which are so important for obtaining the desired musical expression. When I tell the musicians of an orchestra, "downbow," or "upbow," or "use such and such a fingering," everyone knows what to do. In Washington, once or twice they tried to explain to me that what I wanted wasn't possible. So, I grabbed a cello and gave a demonstration. End of discussion!

C.S. Must a conductor be an instrumentalist himself?

M.R. It's not absolutely necessary. But he must be a *musician*, which is much more important. Nevertheless it is useful for a conductor to have experience as an instrumentalist. And by "instrumentalist," I mean "interpreter." A conductor must be able to "interpret" a work even before he stands in front of the orchestra. But the actual qualifications of a conductor are rather mysterious. I'll tell you an anecdote about the power of the eyes. I remember a time when all the instructors at the Conservatory were made to take courses in Marxism. Some of the professors dragged to those classes were old men who had a hard time staying awake. When they were asked a question on Marxism, they looked like they were in great pain. They would struggle: "Wait a moment, it's coming back to me—" Naturally, no one remembered anything. And the old professors' eyes looked like those of dogs who know everything but are unable to express themselves; and that look was enough to satisfy the lecturer.

Now, one facet of man's talent consists of going beyond the level of feeling to that of communication. And this is particularly true in the area of orchestral direction. When an instrumentalist interprets a musical work and offers it to the public, he transmits a finished product which he himself has manufactured, according to his own conception and personal abilities. But when one conducts, one shows the public the way of making others play what one feels. This is very complex. Baton technique is not the only thing involved; the eyes as well as facial expressions enter into it, too. The eyes truly send hypnotic messages. A conductor can keep his hands more or less at his side and still achieve a great deal of expression. I remember a *War and Peace* (Prokofiev's opera) that I conducted at the Bolshoi. During the burning of Moscow, there are some incredibly intense moments; inside, I felt myself so caught up in the music that I couldn't even move. I clenched my fists, and the musicians produced some absolutely wild sounds. At other times when I wasn't quite so taken with the music, I would increase the amount of gestures in order to get the musicians to play more expressively, and the result sounded much less intense. But when I'm there—motionless—concentrating—fists clenched—wow! I get just the right amount of expression without having to make a lot of gestures with my body.

I saw Toscanini conduct the Verdi *Requiem* on film. His hand movements were obviously very clear, but his gestures weren't really ostentatious. As for Furtwängler, I remember seeing him conduct in a film that was aired on television. His gestures weren't at all precise, yet he got the kinds of sounds that no one could have achieved with the clearest and most meticulous gestures.

When I conducted *Eugene Onegin* at the start of my career, I studiously attempted to make my gestures very clear, as I had been advised to do, but the results very often did not satisfy me. That's when I came to understand that there are two kinds of rapport between a conductor and his players: the first kind I would define as direct contact, with the conductor leading so clearly that the musicians, who of course appreciate this method especially, need only follow his gestures to stay together with ease. But each musician makes separate contact with the conductor's gesture; it lacks the sort of "adherence" that pulls the players all together and creates a real ensemble feeling. So, I tried to conduct less clearly, or not clearly at all, and realized that in those moments each musician tried to connect to the person next to him and started to listen—and the resulting sound was infinitely more interesting.

Personally, it irks me when they say either "the conductor led marvelously well but the orchestra played very poorly" or "the orchestra played very well but the conductor led very poorly." The main thing is the sound the conductor wants, and if he gets it, the ways it's achieved are of little importance—whether it's by passing out chocolates before and after the concert, or by having a glass of vodka with all the musicians! When you fly, the important thing is to get from point A to point B.

C.S. With the least possible amount of turbulence!

M.R. Of course, I'm also interested in the quality of the flight. But if the flight satisfies me, I don't worry about whether the captain used automatic pilot or steered the plane with his hands or feet. Such details are not important. The main thing is being comfortable *en route* and arriving at your destination.

C.S. Sometimes, in the concert hall, certain conductors have such spectacularly distracting physical technique—more suggestive of ballet or acrobatics—that whatever the results achieved, as a listener I am prevented from concentrating on the sound produced.

G.V. Yes, I know some conductors who have a brilliant technique and marvelous hands that call attention to themselves. I'm not taken in by them, but they annoy me terribly. So I prefer not to look—but when I close my eyes, I notice how little music the conductor is actually making! And the musicians themselves get frustrated, even if they manage to keep together and make their entrances at the right time.

M.R. I often have the chance to hear cellists, of course, and enjoy listening to them with my eyes closed. It's quite instructive. When I look at them, I follow the movement of the bow and can figure out how the performer feels about the music; sometimes, however, when I close my eyes, the performer's temperament seems to vanish into thin air. But there are also times when, in spite of the flamboyant gestures, the sound retains all its expressiveness. There are no rules, and I repeat: the way it sounds is ultimately all that counts.

C.S. You mentioned Toscanini and Furtwängler a moment ago. I'd like to bring up the case of Leonard Bernstein, the very model of the conductor-dancer-acrobat who still manages to make his orchestra sound wonderful.

M.R. Our ears can tell that Leonard Bernstein has a tremendous musical personality. Even though he's also a composer and a pianist, I consider him an exceptional conductor because he is above all an interpreter. He knows what he wants and one can talk it over with him. And his ideas always interest me.

G.V. Bernstein is never self-conscious. He becomes wildly enthusiastic, leaps, makes flamboyant gestures, but gives his all to the music!

C.S. The way conductors interact with their orchestras sometimes seems incomprehensible. Some scarcely concern themselves with rehearsals and let the miracle occur during the concert. I'm thinking of Charles Munch—

M.R. Munch had a great influence on me. I often spoke with him about the task of conducting an orchestra. On three occasions I had the opportunity to play under him. Sometimes, during rehearsal, we didn't understand each other, but during the concert our minds worked as one.

And since I'm bringing up conductors of yesteryear, I'd also like to talk about Bruno Walter, whom I had the opportunity to meet but never played under. In Los Angeles, I attended his recording sessions of Brahms's First Symphony, and that's when he gave me an autographed photo which I still have.

C.S. What are your memories of Bruno Walter's conducting technique?

M.R. Very mixed memories. As I said, because conductors communicate through gestures, their true musical temperament may be reflected in their everyday behavior. Like man, like conductor! Well, after talking for a quarter of an hour with the then quite old Bruno Walter, I knew he probably conducted with very small gestures. He kept saying, "You understand?" He was someone who couldn't allow himself to make a sweeping gesture, and one could tell this right away, but his limited gestures achieved tremendous results. What's more, he's not the only conductor I've known whose gestures—I'm referring to physical gestures rather than interpretation—revealed his personality.

C.S. Conversely, Galina, do you think Slava's behavior in front of an orchestra reflects his personality?

G.V. I know his true personality better than anyone else and will say frankly that, to me, the Rostropovich of everyday life and the Rostropovich I see on the stage in front of an orchestra are not the same. I have a personal sense of his human qualities, learned over years of our living together, which the public cannot share. When I see another conductor leading an orchestra, I react like any other person in the audience.

M.R. To return to Bruno Walter—he impressed me a lot because he knew how to make the whole orchestra focus their attention on him. He owed this power in part to his reputation. It should be said that a conductor's celebrity has an almost mesmerizing effect on an orchestra. All a great conductor has to do is lift his finger, and the orchestra *must* "do something." If the musicians don't do anything, they understand it's their fault, for that particular conductor couldn't make a mistake! That's why Bruno Walter had no problem conducting an orchestra at the end of his life. Famous conductors encounter fewer difficulties in front of an orchestra than their lesser-known colleagues.

C.S. When one acquires tremendous fame as a cellist and then goes on to conduct an orchestra, how easy is it? Isn't such a person likely to trigger a certain amount of distrust?

M.R. It is much more difficult for a cellist to become a conductor than for an ordinary man. Much more difficult! Because the musicians know that this cellist, or that violinist, occupies a certain position as a soloist, they immediately ask themselves, "Why does he want to conduct? Isn't it enough to play an instrument?" It's apparently not easy to admit that the soloist might have a deep, natural affinity for conducting or seek a new form of expression. In all modesty, but in all certainty, I'll say that if I hadn't already made a name for myself as a cellist, I would have been much more quickly acknowledged as a conductor. More quickly and more easily. But as it is, there is a kind of hostility.

When I direct an orchestra for the first time and start my first rehearsal, I naturally must have them repeat certain phrases. As soon as the musicians understand that my interruptions are justified, they submit willingly. In short, you have to prove yourself.

C.S. But the proof has been around for a long time, and in the most famous places—starting with the Bolshoi, isn't that so, Galina?

G.V. First I'll remind you that I didn't want him to conduct at the Bolshoi!

M.R. That's quite right!

G.V. But, as usual, he got his way. And I knew all the trouble his presence in the theater would give me, but nevertheless I couldn't avoid it. So he began by conducting *Eugene Onegin* at the Bolshoi. He told me he was doing it for me, but frankly I didn't really need it, for I had been singing at the Bolshoi for fifteen years. No, between us, I can say that he was doing it for himself—but he had the right to do so, since he is a great musician who won't compromise the demands of a work. As with everything he does in music, his first production was a complete success, and, ultimately, I was happy about it. We should say that our relationship with the Bolshoi Orchestra was absolutely extraordinary.

M.R. It was a veritable love affair—

G.V. In 1964, after the death of Melik-Pashayev, who for

several years had lent his great personality to the podium of the Bolshoi, the orchestra was really without a head, for none of the conductors who succeeded him possessed the talent required for such a position. So the arrival of Rostropovich was widely considered an event. It should be realized, he was technically still a student; he suddenly found himself at the Bolshoi, never having conducted opera in his life, in front of an orchestra whose every musician had played the same works over and over and knew every note of them by heart. The Bolshoi musicians were so happy to play for him, however, that if he had slipped up or made an error in beating time, they would have helped him out. Their enthusiasm was such that they always would have steered him back on track.

C.S. What about the singers?

G.V. There was a little of everything among the singers! But opera singers obviously aren't used to working with a musician of Rostropovich's caliber.

M.R. I forced the singers to attend several piano rehearsals because I wanted them to sing according to my own conceptions. I never sensed any hostility, but I did encounter some problems, especially with certain individual singers who felt that the height of artistry consisted in shouting as loud as possible. Making them sing *pianissimo* was really the most difficult task of my life. I had to fight!

But as far as the Bolshoi Orchestra is concerned, I must say that I cherish the most exquisite memories, the deepest emotions.

G.V. I think that the Bolshoi players made up the best opera orchestra in the world at that time, thanks to their impeccable technique, high level of professionalism, extraordinary soloists, and in-depth work produced by conductors like Golovanov and Melik-Pashayev. Artistic capabilities placed the Bolshoi Orchestra on a level with the finest symphony orchestras.

M.R. Any comparison is very difficult when the conductors and repertoire are not the same. Personally, I'll never forget the Vienna Philharmonic which I had the pleasure of hearing in the operas of Mozart and Wagner. In that repertoire, the Vienna Philharmonic might claim first place. But nobody plays Russian opera better than the Bolshoi Orchestra.

G.V. All the same, it should be added that, unlike the Bolshoi Orchestra, the Vienna Philharmonic is a symphony orchestra—a symphony orchestra that plays opera. In the majority of opera houses, the orchestra comes second. That isn't the case at the Bolshoi.

M.R. I'll tell you about my debut at the Bolshoi with *Eugene Onegin*. As I had never yet conducted an opera, I didn't know how many rehearsals I would need, all the more since *Eugene Onegin* was never out of the repertoire—but I decided to start from scratch. So I decided I would need the maximum number of rehearsals, and because it was the first number that came to mind, I asked for ten. The management replied that ten rehearsals was out of the question for a work that the orchestra knew by heart, but that they would allow me five. After endless negotiations and a few heated discussions, we agreed upon the number eight. So I began working with the orchestra—and do you know how many rehearsals we had before the first performance? Twenty-two! And it was the orchestra that demanded the fourteen additional rehearsals!

C.S. For what reason?

M.R. Because the musicians were so enthusiastic about the work, because I was giving them new ideas. Actually, those ideas weren't new. They were already in the score. But when

138

one plays a work from one generation to the next, traditions accumulate like barnacles that attach themselves to the hull of a ship and slow it down. Periodically, you have to scrape them off!

G.V. Then there was *War and Peace* at the Bolshoi, which Slava conducted several times. But then all the trouble with Solzhenitsyn started, and Slava wasn't invited back.

C.S. Did you perform together in any other theaters in the Soviet Union?

G.V. I hated going on tour; I never left Moscow. Life in the provinces is so awful! The theaters are so poor! One day I was asked to sing *Tosca* in Saratov. I didn't want to—

C.S. Where is Saratov?

G.V. Somewhere along the Volga. A provincial town. I said, "Let's go! We'll do it together." So the first time Rostropovich conducted *Tosca* was in Saratov. Then, still with *Tosca*, we went to Vilnius, in Lithuania.

C.S. Why do so many mediocre conductors play havoc with operas, often with the very greatest operas?

G.V. For a conductor to express himself in opera, he has to work a tremendous amount with the singers. Under the current system, conductors work very little with the singers. They don't have the time and often don't have the desire either. Even more often, they lack the ability. Young conductors turn up who are poorly versed in opera, who don't know the repertoire, who don't know the meaning of vocal technique. Sometimes it's not a question of conductors not wanting to work, but of not knowing how to work because they have nothing to say. And in the final analysis, they blame it on lack of time. Singers, it must be confessed, generally know more than conductors about performing opera.

As for orchestral conductors, they usually come to the opera house to add an extra laurel to their maestro's crown, to prove their genius, to be the star of the show. In a good production, however, there is no star, neither in the pit nor on the stage; there is only a union of talents—which can be achieved only in a repertory theater with a regular troupe and a permanent conductor. The conductor who dashes in for two rehearsals may be famous and brilliant, but he couldn't care less about what happens onstage. His own success is enough!

Finally, an illustrious conductor blessed with a strong personality is apt to subject the artists to his own personality and, in some way, stifle them. If the singers in front of him are great ones, chances are it will end in a huge dispute, with nobody taking the time to understand each other.

M.R. But then we're not dealing with a great conductor!

G.V. Oh yes we are: a so-called truly great conductor. I know quite well what I'm saying, and I could name names.

M.R. Personally, I often observe that in opera the music is unfortunately relegated to the background. The stagings are analyzed inside and out with no attempt to tighten their true relation to the musical content. And if someone were to emphasize the musical aspect, such an approach would be considered fairly comical. I know that the conductor Temirkanov, the artistic director of the Leningrad Kirov, just did *Eugene Onegin* and staged it himself. I appreciate his talent and, even without having seen it, can imagine how remarkable a performance it is. It means that the music is at the helm, where it should always be.

G.V. He might be an excellent conductor but a worthless stage director and spoil the whole show!

C.S. Slava, I'd like you to tell me about the new turn your conducting career has taken over the past few years—and, more specifically, your love affair with the National Symphony Orchestra in Washington, D.C.

M.R. The National Symphony first engaged me as a cellist, and those initial encounters were excellent. Then I made my United States conducting debut with them, on 5 March 1975. I conducted a Tchaikovsky program, the musicians played remarkably, and we had a great success. It was at this juncture that the orchestra's desire to work with me regularly reached fever pitch. So I devoted myself to the orchestra, made a few replacements among the musicians, and I declare they play better and better every day.

C.S. Your status went from conductor to permanent conductor, which is not really the same job.

M.R. No, there's an enormous difference. A permanent conductor is responsible for his orchestra and plans a large number of cultural events. I devote about eighteen weeks per year to the National Symphony, for concerts, tours, recordings, and the summer season. I'm also involved in planning all the programs and in the hiring of soloists and guest conductors. For example, I know what a certain conductor might or might not be able to do, or what the orchestra will expect of him. What's more, I can focus my own work in a particular direction over a long period of time, and I must say that in Washington I enjoy some extraordinary circumstances, in the area of discipline, for example. Even when I speak softly, everyone hears me because nobody talks, nobody even sneezes!

C.S. Do American orchestras display a particularly strong sense of discipline?

M.R. American discipline is somewhat different from European discipline. But it must be admitted that the German orchestras are very disciplined, and the English ones as well.

C.S. In short, it's the French who are the least disciplined?

G.V. And the Italians!

C.S. Does the work of a permanent conductor also involve shaping the sound of the orchestra?

M.R. Precisely. One can really mold the sound. And you really have to find different sounds for each branch of the repertoire you perform. Can the sound of a Schumann score be compared to a score by Shostakovich? The sound of Shostakovich has to be more intense and the brass brilliant, while too-heavy brass will kill a Schumann symphony, which demands, on the contrary, special attention to the woodwinds.

C.S. Speaking of bright sonorities, and this is a somewhat pejorative judgment, many Europeans feel that American orchestras are bright, and nothing *but*.

M.R. First of all, some American orchestras are not even that! But let's speak of the best: some indeed have a very bright sound, but in reality it's antiseptic. They are remarkable, they can even be perfect, but they lack life. Of the great American orchestras, Boston is the one I prefer. The Boston Symphony is capable of giving truly first-rate concerts. Some are perhaps less successful than others or even completely off the mark, but the vitality is preserved.

142

C.S. And what do you think about European orchestras?

M.R. There are a few remarkable orchestras in London and Paris. But it's obvious that the Berlin Philharmonic is absolutely marvelous. It has been lucky to have had only four permanent conductors; this is a tremendous advantage. But there's another interesting thing to consider: the problem of poor instrumentalists. In every orchestra in the world there are musicians who passed their entrance auditions with flying colors and then received a position in the orchestra, but who later begin to play more and more poorly. In the United States, there is practically no way of dismissing such players from the orchestra because the unions will be right there to defend them. In Berlin, if there's a young upstart who's not playing well, the conductor doesn't even have to intervene: all the musicians themselves will make his life impossible. The players of the Berlin Philharmonic know that their popularity and also their recording activity depend on their level of quality. But orchestras that police themselves out of concern for quality are extremely rare. Experience has taught me all these points.

G.V. Maintaining the level of the orchestra depends greatly on the talent of its conductor. An extraordinary conductor is, after all, a major asset. By the way, when did Karajan take over the Berlin Philharmonic?

C.S. In 1955.

G.V. Naturally it's thanks to that long working relationship that the Berlin Philharmonic has preserved all its qualities. Under such a conductor, how could it have been otherwise?

C.S. Slava, do you intend to remain as long in Washington?

M.R. I'd be terribly old! I don't expect to remain on earth that

143

long! But it's true that a long collaboration between a conductor and an orchestra is an essential point. For the conductor has to know his orchestra through and through. In Washington, I am very humanly attached to my musicians, and I love them a lot. I know when one is ill, I know their problems, I know everything that goes on in the orchestra.

C.S. What kind of relationship should there be between the orchestra and its conductor—one of authority or one of confidence?

M.R. These are very complex relationships, which must first be based on the musicians' total confidence in the conductor. That's a start. This confidence indicates that the musicians acknowledge the absolute competence of their leader and know that it's necessary for them. Next, human confidence enters the picture. A conductor must never offend a musician just because he has indigestion or a headache and feels like taking his anger out on the first available person. Thirdly, it's the permanent conductor's job to provide explanations. The conductor must justify all his actions and make the orchestra understand the meaning behind his decisions. The conductor might naturally disagree with his musicians. Personally, I recall three such cases, particularly the time I didn't share the opinion of a group of musicians about my hiring of a new instrumentalist. I then made my decision but gave all my reasons for it. I explained that our divergence of opinion did not indicate any lack of confidence on my part toward the members of the orchestra, nor even any hostility toward them, but that the qualities of the musician I had engaged were particularly important to us. I showed that it's important to form a coherent ensemble and that taking on an outstanding musician might be harmful if the style of that musician didn't blend in with the ensemble.

144

C.S. Some conductors prefer rather to impose than to explain.

M.R. Yes, there are doubtless many different ways to achieve the same result. I'd rather explain.

G.V. Besides, you couldn't be a tyrant, quite simply because it isn't in your nature!

C.S. I have the impression there are more good orchestras in the world than good conductors.

M.R. Quite right. That's why some very fine orchestras don't attain an outstanding level; it's a level very few conductors allow them to reach. But you need that special sort of conductorial talent and a lot of time for an orchestra to move up a notch. I know several orchestras that currently have the potential, yet haven't achieved the goal.

C.S. Slava, you've always dreamt of conducting an orchestra. And you know that other instrumentalists, some very famous ones, have embraced the same dream. Might it also be Galina's secret ambition?

G.V. Not on your life! I don't like woman conductors. It always looks odd to me for a woman to externalize her emotions, while men can be allowed to do so.

M.R. Yes, what you say is interesting.

G.V. I don't know why, but I don't like to see a woman conduct. Actresses, in fact, express their feelings as a woman. And the different facets of their personalities which they communicate are typically feminine. Yet, in front of an orchestra, in the guise of a conductor, a woman has to ignore her femininity. And that makes me uncomfortable.

C.S. Slava, have you ever played under a woman conductor?

M.R. Yes. Several times.

C.S. And your impressions?

M.R. Well, I don't want to play under a woman conductor again! Because it gives me a very strange feeling. When I play, I obviously look down—and all my life, my left eye has focused on the left side of the conductor's podium. So I never realized until the day of the performance that it was a woman conducting. That day, my eye fell on a high heel, so I automatically looked up. How could it be! It was so different from what I usually see!— Incidentally, I remember a very short American male conductor who also wore high heels, and that distracted me. In all the forty-two years I have been playing cello concertos, I've been used to seeing men's shoes and the end of a pant leg. When the landscape changes, it's a catastrophe!

C.S. Isn't that a bit misogynous?

M.R. No, no, no, no! I, a misogynist? You've got to be kidding!

C.S. If you had to make a choice today between playing the cello and conducting an orchestra, could you do it?

M.R. No, or at least it would be very difficult. I need both. What the cello gives me is the pleasure of direct contact with the instrument and the love of hearing it. But I cannot say that I'm crazy about the repertoire I've already played for so long. On the other hand, as an orchestral conductor, it's precisely the repertoire that fascinates me. I have some tremendous possibilities before me, hundreds of extraordinary works I have never approached. So, between playing the cello and leading an orchestra, between the instrument and the repertoire: don't ask me to make a choice!

146

In Search of a Spark of Genius

C.S. Now for the question that burns on the lips of every composer: Why do contemporary works turn up only sporadically in the repertoire of great performers?

M.R. Before answering that question, I'd like us to reach a mutual understanding of the term "contemporary music." Is it music written by a composer who is still alive? Not necessarily. For my part, I know some living composers who write very archaic music. I've also known some musicians who, at one time, were thought of as avant-garde, but who are now categorized as classicists. I'm thinking of Miaskovsky, whose modernism closely resembled that of Honegger, and whom I considered avant-garde in my youth. Today, he sounds somewhat like Tchaikovsky to me. But music is constantly changing, new trends follow upon each other, and the boundary of what I call avant-garde never ceases to shift.

C.S. Then let's first consider that fluctuating avant-garde, so conspicuously absent from the repertoire of the most famous orchestras and virtuosos.

M.R. The first problem faced by contemporary music is that of rehearsals. A conductor normally maps out his concert programs according to his own chances of success, and how can he be criticized for that? Thus he reserves most of his time for preparing the big symphonic work, which is most likely to show off his talent. This is standard procedure. When he invites a soloist, the conductor tries his best to give him the minimum rehearsal time necessary, preferring to favor his own domain rather than to assure the success of his guest. Thus the conductors who have engaged me, even those who like contemporary music, have always reserved the prime rehearsal time for a symphonic work, sometimes even a contemporary one; and so that I will use as little rehearsal time as possible, they suggest I play the Saint-Saëns Concerto or the Tchaikovsky *Rococo Variations.* Since I've been conducting on my own, I unfortunately have to follow more or less the same rules.

On behalf of the National Symphony of Washington, I've commissioned works from various composers, such as Witold Lutoslawski, Henri Dutilleux, William Walton—and, among the Americans, Jacob Druckman, Peter Mennin, George Crumb, and Gunther Schuller. But those commissions have always involved works for orchestra, without soloist, and those new scores are the ones to which I devote all my efforts before premiering them. Now, we know that audiences are not very likely to go out of their way to listen to contemporary music. So, my soloist is asked to serve a sweetmeat: Tchaikovsky, Liszt, or Chopin—

G.V. Or else the soloist should be tremendously well known, to attract the public!

148

M.R. No, even that wouldn't work. Because, in any case, I don't have enough time to present a world premiere and a contemporary concerto in the same concert, to say nothing of the fact that the public wouldn't be inclined to attend an evening centered entirely around new music.

C.S. The business of sweetmeats leaves me skeptical, because I have the impression that everyone is dissatisfied: those who like classical music and have to swallow a half-hour of new music, and those who appreciate Lutoslawski but hate Tchaikovsky.

M.R. No, I don't agree. I've done a lot of study on this in the United States and must say that, among ticket buyers, there are at least ten times as many Tchaikovsky fans as Lutoslawski fans. The former are the ones I have to persuade, though I'm sure the great talent of Lutoslawski is able to impress them.

For each program with the National Symphony, I'm given four rehearsals. If the musicians go even a minute beyond that time frame, they are paid for overtime, and that's frightfully expensive. To avoid it, I put together a program that stays within the allotted rehearsal time. That's the bottom line.

Let's imagine, for example, that I'm invited to play the Berio concerto *Ritorno degli snovidenia*. To present that properly after two rehearsals is impossible. The dialogue with the soloist won't work well if the orchestra doesn't have the time to understand its own role. So one must schedule extra rehearsals, knowing all along that the public won't be coming in droves to this concert. On the other hand, if I'm asked to play the Dvořák or the Saint-Saëns Concertos alongside a symphonic work by Schumann or Tchaikovsky, tickets will be certain to sell quickly. Yet, contrary to what Galina has said, the soloist's name is not always what counts. I recently took part in a concert devoted exclusively to Khachaturian in

Marseille, and the hall was not sold out. All I needed to do was play a Haydn concerto—something I already had tried in that very auditorium of the Marseille Opéra—and people would have been hanging from the rafters!

Moreover, you have to take into account the differences in the public's taste. Just try playing the Elgar Concerto in England, and you'll be turning them away at the door! But a concerto by Shostakovich will be much more difficult to sell. And it isn't a question of musical worth, for the Shostakovich concertos are not inferior to the one by Elgar.

So, there is not only the problem of rehearsal time, but also of box office receipts. The concert manager naturally has to take into account the high fees he pays to soloists. As artistic director in Washington, I personally feel ashamed when I'm forced to ask for Brahms or Beethoven from a good violinist who has offered to play a remarkable contemporary concerto. But I'm just as caught up in budget balancing, and need to fill the auditorium.

C.S. The subscription system should help you to do that—

M.R. Yes, but we don't move all the tickets through subscriptions, and tickets still have to be sold for each concert. When everything is sold by subscription, I'll be as happy as can be and plan my programs according to my own tastes. But the box office cashiers are equipped with computers that can tell you, five minutes after the start of the concert, the exact number of tickets sold. You always have to take the public into account, and the institutions that donate money to the orchestra. It's impossible to live without them, which obviously is a big impediment in the diffusion of contemporary music.

In the United States, foundations may help fund new commissions. The work is played, reviews acknowledge the event, but when, if ever, will the work be played again? Heroes are needed to bring off this Herculean feat.

As a cellist, I can attempt to set down my own conditions, but I cannot force a highly complicated concerto on a conductor. For example, I might propose to play the Dutilleux Concerto; the conductor asks, "Is it difficult?"

I answer, "To do it well, yes, it's difficult."

A good conductor would suggest, "Will one rehearsal be enough?"

This doesn't discourage me, so I continue to fight for the love of these works. And it's not only a struggle for living composers. To play music even as well known and popular as Prokofiev and Shostakovich, I have to fight, too. I don't have to search for an example: for one of my latest concerts in London, I offered to perform Prokofiev's *Sinfonia Concertante*, and despite my insistence, the administration refused initially. They finally gave in, but why? Because a special rule in London forbids two soloists to play the same work in the same season; the administration's choice for me was the Dvořák Concerto, which another cellist had already put on his program— So I performed the Prokofiev score, the hall was sold out, and the audience enthusiastic. But, unfortunately, concert life today depends above all on computers—

C.S. And things are hardly any more satisfactory in the opera house, where the sums of money invested are incomparably higher—

G.V. It's terribly difficult. To produce a Prokofiev opera such as *War and Peace* is practically impossible. You need fifty performers who, even if they don't have large roles, must be extraordinarily talented. Incidentally, that's what happens at the Bolshoi, where great singers, at the request of the directors, are duty-bound to fill small roles in performances of Soviet opera. Whenever *War and Peace* is produced, the whole troupe takes part in the show.

While I'm on the subject: the Bolshoi is a theater where

you aren't hampered by lack of time. An opera might stay in rehearsal for a year, if necessary. You want eighty orchestra rehearsals? You've got them. All the artists come to rehearse in the morning, as in a factory. If they have to stay longer, into the evening, nobody complains. It's not because the Bolshoi musicians and singers particularly love their art, it's because it's their work. If they refused to do an extra quarter of an hour, they'd have the worst problems with the conductor and, at the first opportunity, would be let go. I must say that on this particular issue I agree with the system.

Prokofiev worked for several years with the Bolshoi and benefited from some exceptional performance circumstances for his works. Unfortunately, he didn't have the same amount of artistic freedom at his command. That's how Soviet composers work. They have at their disposal the finest artists to play and sing their works, and excellent working conditions, but they have to write what the government tells them and respect the ideological line. They're given as many rehearsals as they wish, on that condition. Nothing could be easier, since everyone is paid—however poorly!—by the government. Each country has its problems—

M.R. Indeed, it's the government that dictates the Soviet composers' style. And composers of great talent, instead of following the line of God's gifts to them, very often prefer to follow the line of their career. I'll mention the case of Sviridov, a composer of exceptional talent. He knows how to conform perfectly to the Soviet government line. For example, he writes vocal music on texts of classical poetry, and he has composed an oratorio on an awful text by Mayakovski. At any rate, he's very gifted, and whenever one listens to his music in the Soviet Union, it stands out from the prevailing grayness. You think, Hey, a little spark of genius! But the composers have to be very much on their guard; if their flames burn too bright, they get rapped on the head and have a hard time backing out of the situation.

152

G.V. I've been led to believe that some Western composers have sometimes envied Soviet composers. There are so many composers in the Soviet Union whose existence is insured by the government! But the Soviet government pays only those who work within the correct ideological boundaries. It's the government that decides and the people who pay!

In France, certain composers would perhaps like the State to cover all their expenses, but would the French public tolerate hearing a lot of musical gibberish played or sung to the glory of the president of the republic? You have a new president, new works are immediately written, and it's the French people who pay. Can you imagine? Well, that's exactly what happens in the Soviet Union, and the musical quality of the result is totally second-rate.

C.S. Within such a political context, how were you able to keep abreast of musical trends?

M.R. For a long time, we had no idea what was going on abroad. But when I was a student, Shostakovich introduced us to the music of Mahler. Musical life has always been more advanced in Leningrad than in Moscow, and it was in Leningrad that Mahler began to be played. As for Stravinsky, there was a time when even *his* music was banned. The foreign avant-garde wasn't even considered! It was totally banned, and the desire to get acquainted with it eventually diminished. After the death of Stalin, we imagined we saw a little light at the end of the tunnel. A great interest in new music sprang up, and for the first time we came into contact with the music of Schoenberg and the atonal system.

Today, a few Soviet composers are inclined toward the avant-garde; a number of them are remarkable musicians who are gradually becoming known in the Western world: Denisov, Silvestrov, Sidelnikov, Gubaidulina, to name a few. But public performances of their works are barred in the

153

Soviet Union; they're up against an official wall. The exportation of their scores is dependent on the cooperation of the person in charge of the Composers' Union. They could obviously be sent on the sly—but that might create problems.

C.S. How did your interest in new music get started?

M.R. My passion for contemporary music was initially sparked by my friendships with Prokofiev and Shostakovich. I remember the deep impression *Romeo and Juliet* made on me when I saw performances of it at the Bolshoi. It all started with a pure love of Prokofiev's music and ended in a love of ballerinas.

I have a more specific recollection. One day I heard on the radio a gorgeous cello piece that was unknown to me. At the end of the program, I caught only the name of the cellist: Stogorsky, the brother of the famous cellist Gregor Piatigorsky, who had changed his name for obvious reasons. ("Piatigorsky" means "five mountains," so the brother didn't hesitate to adopt "Stogorsky" as his new name, which means "one hundred mountains"!) So, after having caught a "glimpse" of that cello work, I went to Stogorsky's in the middle of the night to ask him the title of the piece he had played on the radio, and he informed me it was the Adagio from the ballet *Cinderella* that Prokofiev himself had transcribed for cello and piano. I immediately copied down the piece, for it was unpublished, and played it in public shortly thereafter.

When the Soviet government's henchmen tried to obliterate Prokofiev and Shostakovich in 1948, I was shattered. One day, on arriving at the Conservatory, I saw affixed to the wall the decree declaring that Shostakovich had lost his job because his qualifications didn't suit his appointment. That's why I never finished my composition studies: as soon as Shostakovich was chased out, I decided to abandon my courses at the Conservatory.

154

C.S. In a certain way, didn't the Soviet government reproach composers for losing sight of the traditional and nationalistic values of Russian music?

M.R. No doubt. That said, I think an attachment to tradition is a constant trait of the Russian character. Russians don't easily get away from their ancestry. They never want to lose touch with their roots. That's why in the twentieth century, except for a man like Bartók, it's the Russian composers who best preserve their national character. Listen to Prokofiev's First Piano Concerto: this is typically Russian music, from first note to last. It's totally recognizable.

C.S. But when first performed, that concerto was considered awfully modern—

M.R. Because people are so used to harmonic traditions, because they're brought up on classicism. And suddenly, a rocket lifts off!

G.V. How could we continue to write the same music in this day and age? The way we dress, the houses we live in—our whole life is different and our aesthetic demands, too.

M.R. But Russia knew nothing about new music for a very long time. We discovered Webern, for example, only after his death.

C.S. The West did too. On the other hand, some of Schoenberg's works were played in Leningrad in the 1920s.

M.R. As far as Schoenberg is concerned, for the moment I prefer to reserve judgment because, as important as his theoretical contribution seems to me, I question his musical inspiration. No, as I told you, in Russia we contented ourselves with murmuring Mahler's name with deep respect

155

because we knew that Shostakovich was crazy about him; we hadn't heard anything by Mahler but were reading his scores, dazed out of our wits! In fact, for my generation, Western musical history stopped at Wagner. Though we were sometimes told about how avant-garde music had been able to develop in Leningrad for the privileged few in the 1920s, that was only a memory for those of us who were trying to crack open the wall of interdiction.

C.S. A memory of *Wozzeck*?

M.R. Indeed, *Wozzeck* had been played in Leningrad. On one occasion! Even if successful, a single performance passes unnoticed. Yes, perhaps some few actually heard *Wozzeck*, but the others merely recall the event's occurring and the title of the work— It's true that the list of world premieres in the Soviet Union in those times is rather long, but the problem is that works have to live on in repeated performances. There was a sudden burst of premieres at the end of the 1920s. Since then, we've kept to the rearguard. Even as far as Stravinsky is concerned— When Leonard Bernstein came with an American orchestra to conduct *The Rite of Spring*, he declared, "Unfortunately, this work doesn't get played in your country, but we are happy to present your compatriot's work of genius for you." That speech caused quite a stir! "Ah! He wants to teach us a lesson!" They replied that *The Rite of Spring* had recently been performed in Tallinn— First of all, I'm not sure about the quality of the Tallinn performance; next, I can only imagine how many people were reprimanded for that daring deed. And it's only because of the scandal that anyone found out *The Rite of Spring* had been played there at all!

C.S. When Igor Stravinsky returned to the Soviet Union on the invitation of Nikita Khrushchev, he was taken, as soon as he arrived, to a concert where *The Rite of Spring* was being played. Upon returning to Paris, he told me, "Don't quote me, but it was very badly played!"

G.V. I remember the concert, which took place in the auditorium of the Conservatory. We attended it, and it was a very great event for Russian musicians. In the course of my travels abroad, I had never had the chance to meet Stravinsky, so this first contact was moving. At the end of *The Rite of Spring*, the ovations rang out; Slava and I were the first ones to stand, and then the whole audience stood up to salute his return to his native land. I saw him again at the Bolshoi; I believe it was for the performance of *War and Peace* in which I was taking part, and I was invited to his box during intermission to meet him.

C.S. But the era of *The Rite* was already strangely distant, and Stravinsky had been going in some pretty disconcerting directions for half a century.

M.R. Something disturbed his relationship with God. It's difficult to say just when, or to explain how and why. But he lost that absolutely incredible contact that he had with the Lord in the beginning. He did make tremendous advances and remains all the same a composer of genius in every one of his works. I recall what Prokofiev used to say to me: some composers are like mules—they toil remarkably well, but they cannot have children. There are some gifted composers who are like that. They're wonderful, but they have no descendants. Stravinsky opened up new horizons, but I cannot imagine a second Stravinsky.

C.S. Why didn't Stravinsky write a major piece for the cello?

M.R. I asked him that. And Robert Craft* immediately broke

---

*American conductor born in 1923. Close friend of Igor Stravinsky from the 1950s until his death, he played a major role in interesting the old master in the post-Webern serialist style.

157

into the conversation with, "Why? He can write something only if the Soviet government pays him!" Did Stravinsky really need the money?

C.S. Other composers have been more cooperative, and thanks to you the cello repertoire has been considerably enriched. You continue, however, to wrestle and plead with the best composers. Who was the first?

M.R. The first? I always dreamt of contemporary composers consenting to write for the cello, but when I first embarked on my career I was completely unknown and had no way of making contact. My first adventure along these lines was rather strange and tinged with a hint of scandal. Svyatoslav Knushevitsky, as you know, was a talented cellist with an extraordinary tone. He was a marvelous musician, but his Achilles's heel was a weak instrumental technique. In those days, when I was still only a teenager, Reinhold Glière had written a very long and difficult cello concerto and told Knushevitsky he could give its first performance. When Knushevitsky first played the concerto, a really quite perilous piece whose difficulties he couldn't master, Glière was in the audience. So was I, and it was one of the most scandalous concerts I ever attended because the soloist periodically came to a dead stop while the orchestra continued to play— And Knushevitsky would place his pages of music on the floor and start pushing them under his chair with his foot. Glière then turned to me and said, "I want you to play this work the way it should be played!" I replied that I would play the concerto only after Knushevitsky had played it a second time, that he should be given a chance to redeem himself, that his stage jitters and his age should be taken into account, and so forth. I don't remember if he played it again or if he got out of it. But I remember Glière, who was the dean of Russian composers. He could have been friends with Tchaikovsky— Later I played his concerto, and he phoned me to ask for permission to dedicate it to me. That's the first work that was dedicated to me.

C.S. How modern was it?

M.R. Oh, it was in a very old style— Even Tchaikovsky would seem modern next to Glière. As for his concerto, it was terribly long—and there were some interminable dead spots for the soloist. I think it was in the second movement that I had nothing to do for two hundred bars. If I had shaved at the beginning of the performance, my beard would have grown back by the end of the last movement.

I cherish the most marvelous recollections of Glière himself, and memories of several trips, in particular. He would always arrive on the stage covered with medals, which was quite distracting during a concert because they all rattled like a percussion section. He would host very elaborate parties in his home, inviting one or two hundred people; I was invited and tremendously impressed. When I was offered a promotion on the faculty of the Conservatory, I had to present two recommendations. Prokofiev gave me the first one, and Glière the second. While writing his letter, Glière suddenly stopped and shook his head for a long time: "I would have liked to refer to you as a 'genius' but that's impossible; we don't have the right to call anyone that but Stalin."

After Glière, everything began to click. I entered a competition and played the Concerto by Nikolai Miaskovsky, a very poetic work that I dearly love and will surely have the opportunity to return to some day. In Washington, for the composer's centenary, I conducted his Symphony No. 21; it's remarkable music.

C.S. Do you think Miaskovsky's talent is unjustly neglected in the West?

M.R. Yes, in my estimation there is a void as far as appreciation of his music goes. His Fifth and Sixth Symphonies are virtual masterpieces. His music is dark, what I'd call a sort of Russian César Franck. He also sounds a bit like Chausson. He was a close friend of Prokofiev (their correspondence has been published), and he was later part of the group of composers condemned by Jdanov. Miaskovsky was then considered the patriarch of Russian music.

C.S. The first modern music you became acquainted with was Prokofiev's?

M.R. Yes, and when I heard it for the first time it seemed terribly new to me. When Prokofiev composed his *Sinfonia Concertante,* the original version of which I played at the premiere in Moscow on 18 February 1952 with Richter conducting, it was difficult to get authorization to play such music, for we were still experiencing the aftershock of Jdanov's decrees. The premiere of the second version took place later in Copenhagen, after Prokofiev's death, and I had to think up a thousand excuses to get them to allow me to go.

G.V. For me, this brings to mind *War and Peace,* my first Prokofiev opera. It was in the 1958–59 season at the Bolshoi. Ten years earlier in Leningrad, I had been involved in a production of the work, performed in two evenings, but the Bolshoi was presenting it in one evening; Prokofiev never heard it performed that way.

M.R. When he became ill, Prokofiev repeated over and over to me, "I'd like to live at least long enough to hear my *War and Peace* one last time."

G.V. I remember the difficulties encountered in 1947 in Leningrad. The instrumentalists would say, "Oh, this is really an interesting work; there are some nice things in it. You know, there's a remarkable waltz." But the singers had a few problems with it—   Ten years later in Moscow, however, the singers understood everything from the first rehearsal on. The singers began to appreciate the score; working on it was a joy for everybody. Yet only a decade had passed since the premiere.

Then they did Prokofiev's *Story of a Real Man, Semyon Kotko*, and *The Gambler*. The first Soviet opera I sang was Shebalin's *Taming of the Shrew*. But to get back to Prokofiev, I'll say that he always wrote remarkably well for the voice. His language is at once very refined and very logical. Shostakovich's vocal writing is very different, and probably more difficult.

C.S. In any case, it's a difficulty he reserved especially for you, since he dedicated several of his works to you.

G.V. Indeed, the first such dedication was the vocal cycle of *Five Satires* on a text by Sacha Chorny, then the orchestration of Mussorgsky's *Songs and Dances of Death* and the *Romances* on poems of Aleksandr Blok. Next, he composed the Symphony No. 14, which is dedicated to Benjamin Britten; at the premiere, I sang the solo part, which he wrote for my voice.

C.S. The subject of Shostakovich's vocal writing once again brings up the issue of the difficulty of performing contemporary music—

M.R. On this subject, I'd like to talk about the experience I had with the Soviet composer Arvo Pärt who now lives in the West. He's a very talented musician who wrote me a Cello Concerto that I've played one time. It was a very modern work, and Pärt designed a sort of system using little crosses, whereby he indicated the places on the cello that had to be struck by the hand or the bow. Of course, the sound varied according to where the instrument was struck, and I must say that the result was rather musical. But unfortunately I have an intense temperament, so whenever I started to hit the cello, I thought I was going to scratch it. At the time I played it, I wasn't yet using a very precious instrument. But today, nobody could make me treat my Stradivarius like that. One possibility for doing that work might be for me to have two cellos: one to play, the other to strike. That said, instead of asking me to strike my cello, I imagine Pärt could have figured out something for the percussion section, even if it had meant a slight difference in timbre.

I also performed a very modern work by Lukas Foss, another highly talented composer. His idea was to rig the cello with a microphone connected to an amplifier. Little by little, he increased the volume in a phenomenal crescendo. I went crazy. Trombones and trumpets were blaring at the same time, and still I had the wild feeling that my cello was covering the whole orchestra!

Now, there's another crescendo in the finale of the Shostakovich Second Concerto, which reaches a climax; it's a crescendo without a microphone, yet it achieves no less of an effect than the amplified one. Composers naturally have a right to experiment, but sometimes it can all be so much simpler. Yes, I believe in the power of simplicity!

I'll add that there's no such thing as "bad tone." There are simply sounds which suit or don't suit a given work or instrument. When necessary, I myself am capable of producing some atrocious sounds on my instrument, and with great gusto, for any sound skillfully used by a composer can provoke an emotional response.

I've known numerous painters personally, major artists like Picasso and Dali; they used fairly standard colors. One day, I met a Mexican painter named Rufino Tamayo. He showed me how he traces little circles with the cap from a tube of toothpaste, and they're very pretty little circles. I appreciated the effect he wanted to produce and the connection between the material and the artistic project. The same goes for music. If composers feel they need a certain sound, they can produce it boldly. Even in opera, a shout can be interesting if it's uttered at the proper moment. It has the right to exist.

I'll tell you what happened in London during the recording of the Shostakovich opera *Lady Macbeth of Mtsensk*. A highly refined diva was singing the role of Sonya, the prostitute, whom Katerina Izmaylova pushes from a boat and into the water. It should be explained that the scene takes place in Siberia, where it's snowing, and that the water is churning with a very strong current—which is to say her situation is totally desperate. When Katerina pushes Sonya, the latter must howl, howl like an animal.

I had spoken to the singer before the recording session, telling her, "You have to howl as though you were screaming for your life!"

"Okay, I'll try."

"Very well then, as soon as I give the signal, you let out a scream."

And that scream rises above an orchestral *pianissimo* as the double basses and timpani mark a simple beat. I give the signal, she screams and—it was so pretty! But it wasn't effective at all!

I found a solution. I looked at the chorus and saw a young woman with thin lips, lips as thin as paper! And I saw her eyes, which flashed daggers.

"You—let out a scream!"

"I'm afraid of damaging my voice, but I can do it."

"Will you try?"

"And if I ruin my voice, will I be paid for my scream?"

"Of course!"

In the engineering booth, there was an expert sound engineer named Souvi Grabb, an imposing specialist. I said to him, "Prepare yourself! Turn on all the mikes for the scream!" We get to the passage in question, and the chorister shrieked in such a manner, I almost fell over! I ran into the booth and found the sound engineer in tears. I won't say anything about the recording as a whole, but I do advise you to listen to it sometime for the scream alone.

All this is by way of explaining that there is such a thing as an indispensable sound, not necessarily beautiful, but which suits a given passage in a given work. And this is true for the cello: experiments can be made, provided they're gone about in the right way.

C.S. Does this mean that when performers approach contemporary music they always have to rethink their technique?

M.R. For me, it involves a tremendous amount of work. I must say that before studying the Lutoslawski Concerto, I rarely used quarter-tones. And Lutoslawski even uses eighth-tones! They're fairly easy to play on a stringed instrument, but if you've been playing only halftones for thirty-five years, you find yourself having to master a new technique. The new technique at times might appear impossible or insurmountable, especially when it's written down in traditional notation. In my case, I started from scratch and played each note separately, but that wasn't the right method. So I wrote some special fingering instructions on my music, and it all became clear. It is sometimes easier to play this sort of music than it is to play classical works; you just have to know how to go about it.

C.S. Even if they don't seem very practical, don't the new techniques called for by contemporary composers open up rich new horizons for the instrument? I'm thinking of Lukas Foss, whom you've mentioned, or Xenakis, who has written two pieces for solo cello.

M.R. I admit that my interest in playing certain works is purely a sporting one. The Lukas Foss Concerto is technically so difficult on the cello, because of the wide leaps the soloist has to make, that it would be simpler to play it on the piano. For me, it was a game to hit the written notes, or thereabouts— But I wouldn't want that to seem like a negative assessment of the Foss Concerto, for I have no regrets about all the physical effort I put into playing it. It's a work that contains some remarkable elements. As for Xenakis, when I listened to *Nomos alpha* for the first time, I was quite intrigued by its many novelties and curious to know how they were performed. It's a fascinating pursuit, and one day Xenakis may write a cello concerto that follows brilliantly from those experiments—unless another composer, inspired by Xenakis's ideas, writes a tour de force for the instrument first.

This is why I have given the premieres of more than sixty sonatas and concertos, and I well know that less than a quarter of them will stay in the repertoire. But I think any average work, and even a bad work, is likely to inspire other ideas.

Once I had to play a certain Soviet composer's concerto, and I prayed to God that Shostakovich wouldn't attend the concert, but he came— He later asked me, "Could you tell me why you're playing that awful music?" And I stammered, "I don't have time to explain, I'll tell you some other day—" We then went out to eat, and he mentioned to me that as a member of the committee that awarded the Lenin Prize, he had to go to the Vaghtantov Theater that evening to attend the performance of a play entitled *The Cook*. We had a few more drinks and went to the theater together. At the end of the show, I said to him, "Well, now we're even! You wasted your time at my concert, and I wasted mine at this play—" It was an awful play! And Shostakovich was just as disgusted with the music I had played. Sometimes, though, a composer gets another idea in response: by hearing a work that sounds so bad, he suddenly imagines the changes that should be made for it to sound good. That's why I've played so many new, often flawed, scores, with the hope that they might inspire successful works. I've also told myself, God will reward me! If I stick to it, perhaps five masterpieces will be created.

C.S. But does performing all these works, masterpieces or not, require the same effort?

M.R. Every interpreter must muster all his strength to perform a work, whatever kind of work it may be. Playing music, whether good or bad, demands training, self-discipline, deep dedication. Even when I play an inferior piece, I am convinced I love it. I play it with all my heart. But I realize afterward I'll never play it again. The act of concentrating on the work and forcing myself to like it is nevertheless essential in my work as a performer.

I won't single out any one composer, but I play all works with great love, even if that love is sometimes the result of an artificial persuasion. A man marries and then divorces thinking, "I thought I loved her—" but he still got married. Well, there have been works I thought I loved—and later I divorce them.

G.V. My feeling is a little different, for I had an unhappy experience. I had sung in an opera at the Bolshoi that was interesting and successful; its composer then decided to write a song cycle with orchestra for me. I was therefore obliged to sing it. Today I feel I should have refused, but the work was dedicated to me, and the composer was a respected personality, old and in ill health. In short, I sang it. But when I was on the stage, I hated myself and wondered what I was doing there. It was mediocre, nondescript, a not particularly modern piece that spoke of collective farms and agriculture. I sang it in the auditorium of the Conservatory, and since I was well known, I was thinking about all the people who had come because of me. I was ashamed, and my sole desire was to get off the stage as quickly as possible. When I returned to my dressing room, I had a fit of hysterics. I cried because I felt

166

I had acted against my better judgment and good taste. I had lowered myself to sing a work that was worth absolutely nothing! I never did that again!

C.S. I imagine there are composers whom you know well, who are perhaps even your friends, but who don't necessarily have a lot of talent; they ask you to premiere their works. What do you do?

M.R. I cannot tell you how painful it is. Particularly for Galina, since her voice is a gift from heaven. But she has to take care of it and preserve it for performing mainstream works. As for me, no matter how bad the pieces I have to play are—and I have a few in mind—performing them enriches my experience as an interpreter and will perhaps enrich my knowledge of the instrument and my technical skill. There may be in them some detail or other that I can bring to the public's attention. Even if the work is a mediocre one.

I receive more works in my capacity as a conductor than as a cellist. For the cello, they're generally pieces by amateur composers who adore the instrument. I don't know why, but there are a lot of women who play a little piano and next set about writing romances for the cello! It's awful! They give them to me as gifts after my concerts and I think, This is unfair! After all, tonight I gave a good performance!

But, in this "prospecting" for new works, I'm served by an excellent memory, which I thank heaven for giving me. In connection with this, I'll tell you what happened to me concerning Vladimir Vlassov, in the hope that he won't get too angry. Vlassov was a rather average composer who was very nice to me, and since he lived on the same floor as I, proximity made our relationship more complicated: he always had excellent vodka and something good to eat in his apartment— He wrote a cello concerto, heavily influenced by Darius Milhaud, which I performed—a work tinged with humor, the sort of music one would hear in an amusement park. For I don't know what occasion, he wrote a new piece for the cello, and again he wanted me to play it; I had been eating and drinking so much that my mind was really on other things, but he insisted and didn't stop pleading with me: "Come and play my little number!" He was not a very young man, but charming. "Come on, it isn't very long." Finally, on the eve of the festivities, I began learning the piece and—for fun—thought I'd play it by heart. I should say that I had already heard it played by one of my students but had never studied it myself. So I memorized the piece, but the hardest thing was to not forget it. I rushed to the concert and straight onto the stage, without stopping, for if I had so much as said hello to anyone I would have forgotten it all. I played my friend's piece—and back in my dressing room, in the time it took to say good evening to a few visitors, the music evaporated into thin air! I have a good memory, but it's as erasable as slate!

Today, I have a sizeable repertoire as a conductor and a cellist, and it's obvious that I cannot keep everything in my memory. The other day I had to play the Concert-Rhapsody of Khachaturian, which I had last performed exactly seven years ago. When I picked up the score again, it looked like a new work to me, and I panicked, thinking I had forgotten it all. But I worked on it that evening, and the next day played it by heart.

C.S. When a mediocre composer offers to write a new piece for you, do you try to talk him out of it?

M.R. I have a certain way of going about it, but I don't want to publicize it. It's a technique of refusing without offending!

C.S. Do you receive many scores?

M.R. Yes, and I hang on to them all. In any case, ever since a certain misadventure, I no longer throw anything out. It was in Stockholm, where I'd met the composer and music critic Pergament, who died in 1977. He gave me the score of a cello concerto he had written as well as a tape recording, for the work had already been performed. Some time later, he asked me why I hadn't responded, and I told him I hadn't yet had time to look at the score and listen to the tape. Then, instead of getting back to me, he found a solution that was pretty underhanded: he contacted the Composers' Union, explaining that he had given me his score and his recording, that the recording had cost him money, and that I should either reimburse him or return the material. I broke into a cold sweat, for I was sure I had lost everything. Then I started searching and, to my great relief, was able to locate the score and the tape, which I returned to the Composers' Union. Since then, I keep everything I get! Even if I don't have the time to look at it all. But I'm looking forward to a sabbatical: I am setting aside 1984 for very important tasks, including looking over all the scores I've received.

C.S. Do you think a masterpiece may have slipped past you?

M.R. Yes, I won't rest until I sort through them. It flatters me to know that numerous composers are interested in me. But I'd pay dearly for one page of Messiaen.

C.S. You have a special fondness for the works of Messiaen.

M.R. Yes, I must say that Messiaen is a composer after my own heart. I conducted *L'Ascension* in Washington, and the music touched me deeply. I have the impression that Messiaen is one of the most sincere composers. His music totally expresses his personality. Besides, I'm captivated by the extraordinary effect of the prolonged notes and endless sounds in his works. In them, time stands still. I love his slow tempos— I remember rehearsing *L'Ascension*; I thought I had taken one movement too slow, and Messiaen told me very gently: "If you can, take it even slower." I cannot say that the musicians were very happy, but at times there was an otherworldly beauty about it. In *Quatuor pour la fin du temps,* the most intense emotion is expressed by the sustained sound of a cello in a very slow tempo, and by the piano in the fifth movement entitled "Louange à l'éternité de Jésus."

Today, Messiaen is more inclined to massive works like *La Transfiguration de Notre Seigneur Jésus-Christ,* and personally, I'm eagerly looking forward to his new opera, *Saint François d'Assise.* So, he's working on a monumental scale—mystical and monumental—but to me the voices of his *Quatuor pour la fin du temps* are no less effective in translating some very profound ideas, with very reduced forces. As a believer, I pray heaven that he will return some day to a very spare, concentrated music, with a solo cello part, and I'm sure that with his masterful handling of sound in time, he'll create a work of genius.

C.S. Tell us the truth, you who are so close to composers and so interested in the creative process and new textures: haven't you secretly written a few works of your own?

M.R. When I was at the Conservatory during the war, I started to compose. I borrowed ideas from Scriabin, from Rachmaninoff. I was admitted into Shostakovich's orchestration class, and, very red in the face, I played my First Piano Concerto for him. He said, "Slava, it's a wonderful piece!" And I realized that, for the first time, he was telling me an outright lie! I continued to work with him, and—as I said—that was the start of my interest in contemporary music. My attempts at composition then took another direction; I forgot Rachmaninoff in favor of Prokofiev and Shostakovich. Later I even cast my eye toward Stravinsky. But I realized that such choices were symbolic, and that's why I didn't become a composer. As a composer, I would have had to choose one approach and stick to it, maybe would even have had to begrudge other approaches. I know that Tchaikovsky loved Mozart but hated Brahms, that Shostakovich didn't like Tchaikovsky at all, though the latter was one of Prokofiev's favorite composers. Composers have their own likes and dislikes that fall within certain preconceived boundaries, while a genuine interpreter cannot have only one love. Who could imagine one performer playing the works of the same composer all his life? So I can say in all honesty that whatever piece I am playing at a given moment, that's my favorite piece of all. This evening, I'll play Haydn, Schumann, or an unknown work, and the public will buy tickets to hear me. How could I give the audience something I don't adore?

The Golden Age

C.S. Slava, over the years you've probably said everything you have to say about the cello, and I know you don't like to repeat yourself. But I wish you'd speak a bit about this golden age for your instrument, an age of which you are still very much a part. It's quite an event when a cello recital sells out!

M.R. I remember playing to sold-out houses at Carnegie Hall in the 1960s. That was the first time a cellist ever filled a hall. But I also remember several halls that were half-filled or nearly empty. It's true that the situation has improved considerably. I'm not one of a kind: all the great cellists are successful and play in large halls.

I'm not surprised by this phenomenon. It's connected to an expanding of the repertoire but also to the nature of the instrument. For example, I feel that the sound of a cello is much more interesting than that of a violin. Why are violinists more successful than we are? Quite simply because their music is better than ours.

I think playing the cello is physically more demanding than the violin. And, quite frankly, I think the double bass is an even more difficult instrument to play.

C.S. The first cellos were rather primitive instruments. They didn't have endpins and so were used less for virtuoso displays.

M.R. You know, I've had problems finding a spot for it in apartments I've lived in. Today I'm comfortably situated in a spacious place with many rooms, but in my childhood, my father, mother, sister, and I were elbow-to-elbow sharing the same room. One got used to it. One also got used to playing without an endpin.

C.S. It's true that even in the early history of the cello, master-pieces were written. What do the Bach Suites mean to a cellist—those six famous unaccompanied suites which mark the beginning of a whole repertoire?

M.R. They're as the Bible is to a believer. They're really The Book, the foundation of life—more specifically, the foundation of the cello, not the technical but the musical foundation. Because Bach, like Shakespeare, dominated his era and went beyond the strictures of his time. Bach is the cellist's staff of life.

C.S. When you play a Bach Suite, do you feel any one emotion in particular?

M.R. It's the only music I play at home, for myself alone. The performer has a profound sense of the balance of its proportions, but that balance is inextricably linked to emotional expression. And there are so many emotions in the Bach

174

Unaccompanied Suites that they can never be exhausted. They transcend any abstract, intellectual reasoning. One's technique must be perfect, at the service of the musical thought, and invisible, enabling one to forget it's even there.

In music, technique is indispensable, yet at times constraining and at others gratuitous. Russians are by nature competitive: if you succeed, I can too, and maybe better than you. This is probably why Russian circus artists are always so outstanding. In a certain period of my life, I myself was a victim of this tendency; I wanted to play faster than anyone else. I could play *Flight of the Bumblebee* in around forty-eight seconds! I had a friend, a very old colonel, who played a little violin; we two imbeciles—my accompanist and I—would get together with him, and he would time our performance with a stopwatch. Two idiots! But that arose from a strong feeling of competitiveness, a feeling rampant in a Russia where instrumental technique is so prized. I think the same goes for Italy, but it is not so in Germany. It's no coincidence that the champions of flashy virtuosity like Paganini and Boccherini were born in Italy.

C.S. Why do you speak of this passion for technique specifically in connection with Bach?

M.R. I'm not—I'm speaking of it in a general sense. One part of the musical repertoire is linked to technical prowess, one part tends toward the intellectual aspect, and another part depends on the power of emotion. Now, interpreters can perfect each one of these components separately, according to the works they play and to their own abilities. But with Bach, these three components must be in equal proportion. A fantastic equilibrium and much satisfaction—a kind of perfect bliss—is achieved when, in playing these Suites, a cellist avoids the boredom that is induced by less well-balanced music. But one must respect and take into account each of the three facets of this equilibrium. In the past, I used to put too

175

much emotion in my interpretation of Bach, and that was a mistake.

C.S. Why do you say mistake? Who can say which is the true interpretation?

M.R. I draw the truth from the composer's music. Take the opening bars of any work: straightaway they evoke a certain feeling and whet the appetite. The mouth does not water for a hard-boiled egg as it does for borscht! Well, when I see five bars of music, I have my own response, I immediately recognize the main themes, I "salivate" for that work. Would I play with the same passion if the notes said just the opposite? The music contains its own stylistic demands and forces. There is but one law: the original score. Beyond that, everyone has their personal taste.

C.S. The first cellist whose mouth watered over the Bach Unaccompanied Suites was Pablo Casals. It is he who rediscovered this music and created a style of interpretation.

M.R. I'd like to take this opportunity to talk a bit about Pablo Casals. As far as I can remember, my father took a few lessons from Casals, which allows me to consider myself his grandson of the cello. In any case, he was my idol. I passionately studied every one of his recordings, and the day I met him, at a competition in Paris for which he had invited me to serve as juror, was the greatest day of my life. For me, he was not only a model unequaled in the field of the cello, but also an example of a man attached to his country, a man who loved his people and suffered with them.

To get back to the Bach Suites, it's obvious that Pablo Casals created a style. He played Bach with enormous freedom, as few musicians nowadays allow themselves to play. And clearly, from my point of view, he broke the extraordinary equilibrium of this music. He had to break it, and for our own benefit, for that was the only way to make those Suites famous. In Casals's day, Bach could not have made such a breakthrough with the more intellectual approach.

I remember the day when, in his hotel room in Paris, Casals played one of the Bach Suites for me. He sometimes would stop between phrases and peer at me over his glasses to see my reaction, then continue, but very freely. Casals was such a convincing artist that, when he played, one couldn't level the slightest criticism at him. He felt so deeply what he was performing that he captivated you, impressing you with the feeling that his was the only way the music could be performed.

But when one listens to Casals's recordings, the hypnotic force of his personality is missing. It is the same for recordings by Rachmaninoff or Chaliapin: they are remarkable, but eyewitness accounts indicate that the impact of the performances was much greater in concert or in the opera house. The artist's personality and presence play a key role, especially when the interpretation is carried to extremes. Records don't always convey this sense of personality—and when the magnetism disappears, certain elements of the interpretation may seem controversial to us. When you hear certain young violinists trying to imitate the great interpreters, only the controversial elements remain.

C.S. Why haven't you ever recorded the six Bach Unaccompanied Suites?

M.R. I'm not ready.

C.S. That's the answer you gave me fifteen years ago.

M.R. Maybe I'll take advantage of my sabbatical year to make that recording. I'd need to work on them a lot. I still have several questions about Bach—technical ones above all, concerning the phrasing of virtuoso passages. I was very young when I started studying Bach and following the bowings that my teacher gave me. Forty years later, I modified several elements, but I didn't rethink it totally. I sometimes wonder, should I play three notes legato here and two notes detached there? If yes, why? Unfortunately, we don't have Bach's manuscript, only two or three student copies. One of the copies used for modern editions is in the hand of Anna Magdalena. Seeing the original autograph might have given us some precious information. For my part, I'd still like to experiment a bit.

C.S. Wouldn't it have been interesting to record the Suites in 1950 so that you could've seen how your interpretation evolved over the years?

M.R. I did record two of the Unaccompanied Suites, thirty years ago. Sometimes record producers are highway robbers: they take advantage of the fame you've acquired, and knowing that your records sell, reissue old recordings that you renounce. They take one of your recent photos, put it next to a portrait of Bach, and that's all there is to it!

C.S. Is it legal?

M.R. Unfortunately performers have no legal rights in the matter. And some record companies couldn't care less: they're concerned only about making as much money as possible. There's nothing I can do about it!

C.S. Will the recording of the Bach Unaccompanied Suites be the pinnacle of your career?

M.R. I don't know. I don't think about that. It'll perhaps be the fiasco of my career, but I have to do it. And I'll do it with the sincerity that I pour into all my interpretations.

C.S. After Bach, there's nothing. Why did the classical and romantic composers write so little for the cello?

M.R. I'll know the answer to that later, when I'm able to talk with Mozart—and then I'll let you know. As for an immediate response, can I speak for the composers? Sticking to my own experience with them: when I played the Sonata in C major by Prokofiev, he immediately began composing his *Sinfonia Concertante*. And when I played the *Sinfonia Concertante*, he set about composing the *Concertino*. Before he finished the *Concertino*, he had already embarked on his Sonata for Unaccompanied Cello, though he died before finishing it. Benjamin Britten is a similar case: he wrote the Cello Sonata, then the Cello Symphony, followed by three Unaccompanied Cello Sonatas. I take that as a personal compliment. If I had played the Cello Sonata poorly, would Britten have written his Symphony for me? I imagine if a cellist had been able to inspire Schumann with his playing, Schumann wouldn't have stopped after composing only one concerto!

C.S. So you blame your colleagues, the musicians of past history?

M.R. Yes, in a certain sense, I blame them. But one cannot very well criticize their playing at this distance. I do think that if they weren't able to assert their talent in Mozart's day, it would have been in their best interest to sell their instruments and give the money to Mozart, who needed it so badly. And I blame all the cellists contemporary with Mozart and Brahms for not having inspired any new works by showing the richness of their instrument to the great masters of the day. Good composers have to be entreated, one must humble oneself before them. They must write—anything at all—but they must write! If cellists wrote less music and the great composers wrote more, we'd really be living in a golden age!

179

C.S. In the world of string playing, precious instruments like the Stradivarius are the dream of today's musicians. But for a cellist, is the quality of the instrument all that important?

M.R. It's not so important, unless you perform on a great stage. The instrument and the quality of sound make up your texture. Texture can be aesthetic and create a quality of emotion all by itself, but the main thing is content, whatever you are spelling out. You can express it in a rather twisted manner if your thought is strong. An instrument, even a mediocre one, can be transcended by the strength of an interpretation.

C.S. What was the first instrument you owned?

M.R. It belonged to my father, and I started using it after his death. I don't exactly know where he got it. That was my instrument when I entered my first international competitions and played in Prague. Then I played on an Amati cello I borrowed from a State collection, but I soon understood that a cello is like a spouse: it must belong to you; it cannot be borrowed from time to time. So I returned the instrument to the government.

Next I bought an Italian instrument, a Lorenzo Storioni, made in Cremona around 1760. I used it for a number of years, and Olga is playing it now. With that cello, I made my career. I sometimes borrow it from Olga to give a few concerts and always play it with the greatest pleasure. As for my latest instrument, it's my Stradivarius, the Duport.

C.S. Is it difficult to find and to acquire as prestigious an instrument as that one?

M.R. It's known who owns the great instruments; they are put up for sale only under exceptional circumstances, such as a death or an abrupt reversal of fortune, for an instrument of that quality becomes a member of your family. Giving it up without a valid reason is like committing treason, especially if it has been associated with a major portion of your career.

C.S. When a cellist switches instruments, is his playing apt to change?

M.R. Yes, and that's why one should change instruments whenever one has the chance. It keeps you fresh and allows you to fight against mechanical playing. With a new instrument, I adopt a new comportment. Just try to make the same declaration of love to two different women! What works with one won't work with the other. For each of them, one has to come up with new words.

C.S. And you also play a modern cello built by Etienne Vatelot.*

M.R. When I think of that man I get carried away. We're four friends, Vatelot, Stern, Rampal, and I, our own little jazz ensemble, a jazz quartet. Why jazz? Because it's more fun! Vatelot is an absolutely extraordinary person. He has so many talents! Above all, he's the doctor of our instruments. What could be more valuable? I've never been afraid of death for I know it's inevitable; I fly from one continent to another like a madman and never feel the least apprehension, but I live in constant fear for my cello. If it were damaged in an accident, or if it were to disappear, it would be a tremendous loss for the world. That's why the doctor for this sort of instrument plays such an important role. You have to trust him 150 percent. He must be human and totally honest. My faithful friend Etienne Vatelot has never lied to me, even to spare me bad news.

I was still a poor cellist from the Soviet Union when I brought Vatelot an Italian instrument I had just purchased.

---

*French instrument maker born in 1925.

He sensed I was on tenterhooks, for the origins of my instrument didn't really match the claims of the former owner. It wasn't easy for him, but his honesty was such that he had to tell me the hard truth.

What remarkable talent, what knowledge, and what intuition one must possess to offer such infallible expertise! In this sense, Etienne Vatelot is a unique phenomenon. His ear is unerringly acute, he always gives us the best advice, and he has a sixth sense that makes him absolute ruler over the clinic where we entrust our instruments to him. He even provides an emergency service, which arrives faster than an ambulance with a siren. For my part, I cannot imagine my life as a cellist without Etienne Vatelot.

C.S. And "the Vatelot"?

M.R. Yes, I play the instrument he built for me with the greatest pleasure. There is a certain amount of prejudice against modern instruments; some people swear by the old Italian instruments exclusively. But I give you my word that I played the Vatelot in Marseille recently, and at the end of the concert a musician came up to me and said, "Ah! The famous Stradivarius!"

C.S. When recounting your youthful ambitions, you claimed you could have gone into any trade. Would you like to have been an instrument maker?

M.R. I cannot imagine myself as a luthier. I never would have finished an instrument because I wouldn't have been satisfied. When I give a concert, I try to play the best I can, but I know that even if I play badly, I'll finish my piece. I won't "break" it like I might break a cello I made and wasn't content with. Making a cello is like painting a picture or composing a piece of music. One can always change it or touch it up. When I give a concert, it's finished, I cannot do it over or add anything. It's another form of artistic endeavor, but my approach is mapped out for me. In a field where revision is possible, I'd always want to start over, I'd never accept the end result as definitive. And that is not my sphere.

C.S. Could you give any advice to young composers interested in the cello?

M.R. Yes, one single piece of advice: write! Take advantage of this period in time when the cello is at the crest of a wave. But take into account the instruments used around it: to me, the enormous repertoire for cello and piano duet is terribly artificial. The cello produces prolonged tones, whereas the sound of the piano is percussive, which is to say that after the hammer hits the string, the sound gradually fades away. In short, it's a very different sonority, and putting these two instruments together is not natural. But I imagine the piano and cello will always be together, for composers have gotten used to placing the single voice of the cello against the multiple voices of the piano.

In Russia, as I said, I went on some tours with an accordionist. Frankly, I think the sonority of the accordion is better suited to blending with the cello than the piano is. As far as improving the cello repertoire, there is still much to be done—many advances to be made and many experiments to be undertaken.

The Trials of Tatiana

C.S. Galina, you've had a chance to tell us about the early days of your career—this need to sing, evident since your childhood, and the experience you gained performing in operetta. But your career really took off at the Bolshoi and I imagine that the Bolshoi, in your childhood, must have seemed a sort of crazy dream, the one theater you must have aspired to—

G.V. I cannot say I ever intended to audition for the Bolshoi; my first engagement was a stroke of pure luck.

C.S. Luck?

G.V. Yes. I was strolling along the streets of Leningrad when I saw a poster. Two or three artists, singers and pianists, were traveling from town to town all over the country, auditioning young singers for an invitational entrance competition to be held later in Moscow. So I'm walking down the Newski and find myself in front of the Actors' House, where a poster that says something about "apprentices of the Great Theater" [Bolshoi means "great theater"] catches my eye. I didn't really understand the word "apprentice," and some passers-by explained to me that young singers were being recruited there for a two- or three-year training period. At the end of the apprenticeship, they would either be let go or kept on. I thought, Why not go in and listen? I entered the hall, sat down, and found myself surrounded by young singers, students of the Conservatory; some of them had good voices, though to me they seemed very raw and unskilled. They didn't yet have the artistic craftsmanship that I, through experience, had already acquired.

I felt the level of singing was quite average—singing on pitch seemed to be enough to get the attention of the emissaries of the Bolshoi—so I decided to try my luck too. It was the last day of the auditions, and the jury would be leaving that night. Naturally I wasn't registered, but I was told to come back at four o'clock anyway. I ran to my teacher's to warm up my voice, and without even taking the time to go home, I went back to the hall to sing the Nile Scene aria from *Aida*. I was told, "You must come to Moscow. You'll receive a telegram summoning you." A week later, I got the telegram, entered the Moscow competition, and was the only singer in the entire Soviet Union to be accepted!

C.S. What was the competition like? Did you have to sing certain works?

G.V. No, we sang whatever we wanted, even Italian or German arias, though we had to do them in Russian. The candidates who sang arias without high notes were asked to interpret another piece. But by choosing *Aida*, I knew that I wouldn't be asked to sing anything else, for *Aida* has everything: low notes, high notes, you name it!

186

C.S. Were there many people auditioning?

G.V. There were more than a hundred of us the first round. Men and women. But there was only one adventuress like me: I had never heard *Aida* in the opera house or sung it with a conductor! Now, the second round of the competition took place with an orchestra, under the direction of Kondrashin. He conducted with his eyes, with his hands, with everything he possibly could. When I saw him scowl, I closed my eyes and thought, Catch up with me when you can!

So at both rounds I sang the *Aida* aria, one of the most difficult in the entire repertoire, but I knew right from the start I was going to make it. I had to win at all costs. Win or die! An hour later, they announced the results.

C.S. And that's when the Bolshoi gave you your first contract?

G.V. No, in our country the system is different: one doesn't sign a contract. They start with the most important procedure: they investigate you!

There's a twenty-page form to fill out, and the results must be lily white. So I waited two or three months, the time it took to verify my curriculum vitae: Was I ever in prison? Was I ever outside the country? Was any member of my family in prison? And on and on. Don't forget that this was 1952, and Stalin was still alive. He died in 1953, a few months after my Bolshoi debut.

C.S. What is your earliest memory of the Bolshoi?

G.V. I was just a kid, really, when I arrived at the Bolshoi. I discovered a theater filled with important people, prima donnas everywhere with medals on their chests and big rings on their fingers. It was a time of pompous traditions; everything there was monumental, everything moved slowly, and even in the corridors one walked with solemnity. Sometimes Stalin would be seated in a box. The Bolshoi was truly a court theater.

Then I swept in like a tornado and started to shake the place up. Coming from an operetta troupe, I had another concept of the theater and approached the great operatic roles differently, which in fact corresponded to the changing expectations of our audience—movie-goers, and then television viewers—who no longer settled for listening to opera with their eyes closed.

C.S. What sort of relations were there between the Bolshoi and the State in those days? Were there any political commissars?

G.V. Obviously, and that hasn't changed. Each group in the Bolshoi, whether it be the chorus, the singers, or the orchestra musicians, has its own Party secretary chosen from its own members. Above them, there's a secretary-general for the whole theater.

C.S. Who doesn't necessarily know anything about music?

G.V. Who, necessarily, doesn't know anything about it. In fact, his mission consists exclusively of addressing Party concerns. But there's another authority who, ultimately, has the last word: that's the personnel chief, a K.G.B. officer who has several people working under him. His duty is to verify investigations and keep an eye on the behavior of each artist. No one can be hired by the theater without his permission; no artist can travel abroad if he's opposed to it.

C.S. Do they ask artists, did they ask you, to join the Party?

G.V. Oh, yes!

C.S. And what did you do?

G.V. I always invented good reasons for refusing. I'd say I had no one to do the housework. I'd cry my eyes out explaining I had to go home to take care of the children and cook the meals. So they'd tell me to calm down, and they'd leave me alone. Of all the artists at the Bolshoi, I'm the only one who never once, in twenty-three years, attended the political instruction class that took place every Tuesday.

C.S. What was the working atmosphere at the Bolshoi like in those days? Was there a lot of rivalry and scandal, as in all the great theaters of the world?

G.V. It's precisely in Soviet theaters that the most revolting scandals one can imagine are concocted. Here in the West, scandal is normal: it's the competition game. Every soprano leads her own career: one day *Traviata* and the next week *Butterfly*. One time in London and another time in Paris. Each artist has an infinite number of possibilities. In our country, in the Soviet Union, all the best artists are found at the Bolshoi. For example, when I came to the theater, five other sopranos occupied the same position as I. And there were seven Tatianas, even though *Eugene Onegin* was being put on only once a month. So one soprano would sing the role while the others would find themselves waiting months at a time for their chance. That was the case for the whole repertoire, and that's why young singers who came to the theater were severely handicapped if a great star was in front of them. After all, once accepted by the Bolshoi, they weren't going to sing in the provinces, and of course there was no possibility of their traveling abroad. So they would get impatient and angry, waiting for the star to come tumbling down. For years, quite against my will, I was the brick wall for all the young sopranos.

I sang as much as I wanted but limited my activity to three productions a month. One month I'd be Aida and Tatiana, and all the other sopranos would be sitting around waiting. The following month would be more or less the same. Perhaps there'd be another singer with me, just the two of us, while all the others would again be sitting around. They were still young, but already retirees.

C.S. By virtue of their financial situation and the advantages they enjoy, are Bolshoi artists the privileged class of the Soviet regime?

G.V. Obviously, for the Bolshoi is really the pinnacle to which all Soviet singers aspire. And what's true for singers is also true for the orchestra players, who are paid roughly the same salary. It's a rule that was established under Stalin, and it explains why the Bolshoi Orchestra was, without a doubt, the foremost opera orchestra in the world. It's the theater that attracts the most remarkable musicians of that immense country. Where do the top students of the Moscow and Leningrad Conservatories go after finishing their studies? To the Leningrad Philharmonic Orchestra, the Moscow Philharmonic Orchestra, and the Bolshoi.

To be engaged there is a guarantee of quality and attracts the most gifted individuals. Also, since the Soviet Union is such an insular nation, the finest Russian conductors have appeared at the Bolshoi—at any rate until the death of Melik-Pashayev in 1964. Suk, a conductor of Czechoslovakian origin, Pasovsky, Golovanov, and Samosud—a whole series of amazing conductors devoted themselves to the theater. The orchestra at the Bolshoi was then a superior ensemble thanks to its traditions and the artistic capabilities of its members. But today that's all over because those great conductors are dead. The principal conductor of the Bolshoi is now a certain Simonov. I know him because he arrived while I was still there. One of our Furtseva's blunders, he has truly immortalized himself at the Bolshoi by his feats. The only reason she appointed this Simonov to the position of principal conductor was because his name sounded Russian and not Jewish; the name of the principal conductor of the Bolshoi must bear a Russian name, never a Jewish one (it seems he was half-Jewish anyway). He had just completed his studies at the Leningrad Conservatory when he was engaged at the Bolshoi. I personally couldn't sing with him. I tried to once, but I couldn't even bring myself to look at him. Next to the conductors I have known, he was such a nobody that I absolutely could not tolerate him. I could see the orchestra musicians themselves were so disgusted, *they* didn't look at him. What a nonentity! What must have become of that orchestra by now? I don't even dare imagine. But Simonov was a Party member, young, and bore a Russian name. That gave him the right to annihilate that orchestra.

C.S. Does a Bolshoi artist earn more money than a factory worker?

G.V. As you know, in the Soviet Union they always try to narrow the gap so that everybody makes more or less the same salary. A factory worker doesn't earn any less than the average singer at the Bolshoi, but the Bolshoi artist has other advantages. Not only is the salary about twice as much as one would earn in a provincial theater, but one can have a vocation outside the theater, giving concerts. And above all, artists at the Bolshoi work under the eye of the government, make contacts, and manage to get an apartment. Those are of course great advantages. They are awarded titles that give them a certain status in the eyes of the people; they become "artists of the people of the Soviet Union." So, they are invited all over to give concerts, and they travel abroad.

C.S. When an artist wins the Lenin Prize, is it an honor only, or does one receive a sum of money?

G.V. It's monetary, and on a Soviet scale it's a large sum. The Lenin Prize can go as high as seven thousand rubles.

C.S. As a star of the Bolshoi, you were given permission to sing abroad. When did you first begin to travel?

G.V. If one counts my trip to Prague as a journey abroad, it was in 1955. Next, I went to East Berlin and Finland. But my first capitalist country was England, in 1958. It was in London, during a week-long Soviet art festival in which Slava, Gilels, and Kogan took part, that I performed for the first time in the West; I sang Tatiana's Letter Scene with Kondrashin conducting.

C.S. Being in a capitalist country for the first time must have produced a certain culture shock!

G.V. No, not really. I was there to work and not to sightsee. Soviet artists don't generally arrive until the eve of their performance. All their attention is concentrated on the performance; once it's over, they leave.

My first visit to the United States was in early January 1960. It was during the tour of the Moscow Philharmonic that Kondrashin was conducting, and I was the soloist. My first time in Paris was in 1958, following my trip to London. We were asked to give a concert at the embassy. I went back to France for some concerts, and in 1962 I sang *Aida* at the Paris Opéra. I also sang *Aida* at Covent Garden and the Metropolitan Opera.

C.S. But not at La Scala?

G.V. No. At La Scala I sang *Turandot* and, on the Bolshoi tour, the operas of Prokofiev: *War and Peace* and *Semyon Kotko*. But it was naturally *Eugene Onegin* and *Pique Dame* that I sang abroad most often with the Bolshoi troupe.

192

C.S. What's going on tour like for a Soviet artist?

G.V. It's a very difficult job. I never went on tour in Russia and, other than Moscow and Leningrad, could scarcely name any other cities I sang in. Abroad, other than with the Bolshoi, I always preferred to give concerts, because it's very nerve-racking and unrewarding to be part of a new production each time, with colleagues you've never met before. Such work depends on circumstances beyond one's control, whereas in concert I feel truly responsible for my own actions.

The absence of permanent companies is a big problem in the West. Four soloists arrive at the theater without ever having met and must sing together! When I sang *Aida* for the first time at the Metropolitan Opera, we had rehearsals, but the cast would change over the course of six performances. One day when I walked on the stage, I noticed that I didn't recognize my Amneris. I stared at her: it was a different singer. I had a big scene with her, yet the switch had been made without my being informed! How is this possible? Even a big fee wouldn't tempt me to go through that again!

C.S. The same for the stage director, I suppose. But I have a feeling that certain kinds of stage directors disturb you a bit.

G.V. That's true now, because for years I worked with a stage director of the highest caliber, Boris Pokrovski, whose equal I've never encountered. He obviously had the advantage of a permanent troupe, which is very important, for a stage director doesn't create in the abstract, but has specific artists in mind. Here in the West, the stage director knows that the original cast will give way to a second and then a third. So he divides the scene into a series of little boxes where he places whichever artist may be singing, without taking individual personalities into account.

To say nothing of stage directors who practice innovation for the sake of innovation— For my part, I feel that if

Gounod had wanted to see his *Faust* done in Hessian cloth and pieces of metal, he would have written other music. It's not worth tampering with works of genius. Instead, we should ask ourselves what composers were thinking of while composing them. And simple honesty requires respecting that context.

C.S. When you don't agree with the stage director, what do you do?

G.V. I do what I want and don't waste my time arguing with him.

C.S. And if he argues?

G.V. He can always argue, but I don't respond!

C.S. Does that mean that, all told, you question the whole point of a stage director?

G.V. No. They can be very useful if they manage to convince me that whatever they say is better than what I'm doing. Then I go along with it happily, for I'm always searching for new ideas; I want them and need them. But meaningless changes, like being told to enter stage right rather than stage left: what's the purpose?

That said, Western stage directors do have excuses. When they're asked to prepare an opera in two weeks, as was the case at the Paris Opéra for *Eugene Onegin,* a work nobody knew and the orchestra had never played, what do you expect them to do? They settle for just telling the singers where to stand.

C.S. Insufficient preparation—is that the main criticism you have of opera houses in the West?

G.V. No, I'm not criticizing them at all, I'm sorry for them! They are not able to function properly, and everyone tells me it's because they lack funds.

On the other hand, at the Bolshoi everything is possible. The singers are practically forbidden to leave and don't make fortunes, but they have lots of rehearsals. They might rehearse one opera for six months. Singers in the West get very high fees, and opera administrators figure the artists will refuse to take on more rehearsals for the same money.

C.S. Do you consider the fees in Western opera houses to be excessive?

G.V. No, because I accept them myself, and with pleasure. But I'd like to have both the money and the necessary rehearsals. When we did *Falstaff* at the Bolshoi, we had 260 stage rehearsals. One might well question the purpose of so long a time, which in fact indicates an inadequate level of professionalism; after so long a time, it's like trying to teach an elephant how to dance! The drawback of the system is that very few new productions get done, and a quasi-governmental importance is attached to each one of them. If a production flops in the West and tickets don't sell, it's taken off the bill. Money is lost and that's the end of it. At the Bolshoi, the production remains, whatever happens. Anyway, how could it fail since the political administrators keep an eye on its every detail, and all the more sharply when it's a new opera.

C.S. You often took part in new productions at the Bolshoi—

G.V. The first premiere I did was *Fidelio,* which was also the first opera I sang at the Bolshoi—in Russian, naturally. In fact, Beethoven's opera had never been done at the Bolshoi—nor do I believe it had ever been done in the Soviet Union. And I knew nothing about the role; I had never seen the opera and had never even heard it. But for a young singer, it was truly a monstrously difficult role that demanded a very high tessitura. For an inexperienced voice, it was very dangerous. Maybe it was because I didn't know the work and was unaware of all the trials that a singer encounters that I threw myself into it. And it was while singing Leonore that I figured out how to sing without ruining the voice and how to pace myself. I learned how to sing without screaming. If I had forced the voice, I wouldn't have made it through the performance!

C.S. Is that an experience that can be taught in a conservatory or must one acquire it on one's own?

G.V. No, no, only on one's own. How can you be taught in a school what you must be on the stage to learn? When I arrived at the Bolshoi, I had already acquired a great amount of theatrical experience by performing operetta; I was able to sing while moving around, I no longer had excessive stage fright, and I was already a professional actress. And initially, that's what interested the conductors as well as the stage directors. I had the chance to debut with Melik-Pashayev and work eleven years with him, beginning with *Fidelio* and ending with *Traviata*. As soon as I got to the Bolshoi, I became his favorite soprano. The best years of my life were spent in collaboration with Melik-Pashayev!

As for Pokrovski, he was the number one stage director at the Bolshoi in those years. He had a long tenure there and accomplished a tremendous amount of work. His talent lay above all in his ability to work on a role and create an in-depth characterization. He knew how to bring out the acting potential in each artist, qualities the artist might not even know he had. I never met another stage director of the same caliber. I can truly say that my debut at the Bolshoi occurred under some absolutely fantastic circumstances!

C.S. Do you have any specific recollections of that first *Fidelio* at the Bolshoi?

G.V. Obviously, in our country, in the Soviet Union, *Fidelio* was done as a political, revolutionary production. The text was changed, primarily to treat the subject of liberty and mankind's pursuit of happiness while de-emphasizing the personal drama of the two protagonists. The result was a grand operatic machine glorifying Florestan's heroism. As for me, I played a very energetic young girl, very romantic, very much in love.

C.S. Beethoven is often criticized for composing music better suited to the concert hall than the opera house.

G.V. That's not true. *Fidelio* is absolutely an o-p-e-r-a! Leonore is a fantastic part, and having just seen the horrors and endless sufferings of war, I was captivated by the character. I believed I was going to rally everyone and everything over to my side, that entire regiments were behind me.

C.S. Did the Bolshoi audience like it?

G.V. Who is the Bolshoi audience? The public was not concerned. *Fidelio* was being done for the first time, and the professionals came to acquaint themselves with Beethoven's opera. But the production wasn't intended for the average, run-of-the-mill, ordinary public. Besides, the notion of a Bolshoi "audience" is a little odd. The tickets are always sold out, and there's always a long line at the box office, but the average Muscovite goes infrequently to the Bolshoi. Those who have occasion to attend once probably won't go back again for the rest of their lives. The Bolshoi audience consists mainly of people passing through, people on a mission. That is to say, the audience's level of appreciation is particularly low. They come, look at the set, leave, and never come back; if every inhabitant of the Soviet Union came to the Bolshoi once in a lifetime, that would be enough to fill the house every night. But naturally, it's very unhealthy for the house to be filled for reasons having nothing to do with the production or the cast. What's more, the repertoire of the Bolshoi is planned to please everyone, from the factory workers to the academicians, who are favored with complimentary tickets. What stupidity!

C.S. And that no doubt explains the highly conventional character of the Bolshoi productions seen in France—

G.V. What you have seen is, indeed, typical of the Bolshoi style. *Prince Igor, Boris,* and *Khovanshchina* have been performed with the same sets and costumes for forty years!

C.S. In spite of all this, the Bolshoi represents the peak of Soviet operatic art?

G.V. Yes, it's the zenith. "Artist of the Bolshoi" is truly an important title. As for the other houses, there are perhaps around forty of them, but they're rather average—except for the Opera of Leningrad and those of Vilnius, Tallinn, and Riga. The Baltic countries remained independent until the war and preserved a cultural tradition. There, they even do Wagner and Mozart.

C.S. Whose works are not performed at the Bolshoi?

G.V. I've sung *Lohengrin* and *Tannhäuser,* but only in concert version. In my day, they didn't stage Wagner at the Bolshoi. I recall only a *Flying Dutchman* done in the 1960s, which was withdrawn after two years. Mozart doesn't fare any better; they did only *Le nozze di Figaro,* and I sang Cherubino.

C.S. Was that your only Mozart role?

G.V. Yes, I'm sorry to say. Now that I've lived a few years in the West, I infinitely regret not having defected twenty years sooner. So many roles passed me by— So many lost opportunities due to the Bolshoi's limited repertoire! One could go crazy singing the same role for twenty years!

C.S. Did the Bolshoi management force you to? Weren't you free to choose your roles and colleagues?

G.V. It all depends. At the Bolshoi, the amount of leeway depends on the celebrity of each artist. Personally, I always chose my colleagues. The management let me. If there was a problem and I really couldn't refuse the authorities, I'd go to the doctor, open my mouth, and say, "I have no voice." And he'd give me a medical excuse. All the great singers of the Bolshoi did the same thing. The doctor wasn't taken in by it, but he never would refuse. For if I went on and actually had a problem during the performance, I could always say, "I consulted the doctor and he claimed nothing was wrong with me." It was in his best interest to issue a medical excuse, no questions asked, rather than to risk losing his job for good.

C.S. When you first came to the Bolshoi, did they give you small roles?

G.V. No. At the Bolshoi, young singers are engaged for a trial period of one year, and during that period they are given one leading role. That's when the conductors and stage directors observe the debutantes and decide either to integrate them into the company or to let them go. I myself was lucky enough to start out at the Bolshoi in two leading roles: Leonore in *Fidelio*, which I've already told you about, and Tatiana in *Eugene Onegin*. My destiny is closely linked to Tchaikovsky's opera. *Eugene Onegin* has crossed my path all my life, not only from the start of my career but from my childhood as well. And Tatiana served as my operatic farewell at the Paris Opéra.

C.S. In your opinion, what special place does the role of Tatiana occupy in the operatic repertoire?

G.V. I'll say first off that she's a totally Russian character. All our women are Tatiana, or Liza in *Pique Dame*, both Pushkin characters. Children study Pushkin in school and they all know who Tatiana is. Later, all Russians encounter Tatiana in the theater or in the opera house. Tatiana is a part of their culture, even if they don't know the music. For them, Tatiana is an icon of femininity, purity, sincerity. No other role combines these three qualities so harmoniously.

For a singer, Tatiana is a very special role. Singing it prettily or seductively is not enough. The interpreter must truly enter into the character, plumb her depths, get right under her skin. A Tatiana must accept the idea of sacrifice, as if that sacrifice were as natural as love. For a Tatiana, love is forever, and she endures its inevitable trials without flinching. Many Russian women resemble Tatiana. And Tatiana is the Russian woman: not a lady of high society or a poor peasant girl, but Russian Everywoman.

C.S. Does that mean you yourself are a Tatiana?

G.V. Indeed! Not only does the character of Tatiana fit me like a glove: it's in my blood. I have dreamed like Tatiana, I fell in love like she did, and—like hers—my first love was unhappy. I was ten years old— An artist who interprets Tatiana must pretend nothing. She must simply get inside Pushkin's poetry, listen closely to the music—and sing.

C.S. What about Liza, Tchaikovsky's other famous heroine?

G.V. Liza is equally Russian, but she's a troubled character. She has broader social horizons. Tatiana is a country girl whereas Liza is the heiress of an important family in St. Petersburg. Her love scene with Hermann indicates this: she

200

is different from Tatiana, more free and headstrong. She determines her own destiny.

C.S. As for Mussorgsky, he unfortunately wasn't thinking of your voice when he wrote his operas—

G.V. Alas, no! However, I did sing the role of Marina in *Boris Godunov,* which is written for a mezzo. I didn't sing it on the stage but for a recording conducted by Karajan. Marfa in *Khovanshchina* is a role I have very much yearned to do, but that's a mezzo part too.

C.S. Is it frustrating not to have the voice for a role one would like to sing?

G.V. Of course, but one must learn to discipline oneself. At the Bolshoi I was able to sing whatever I wanted. If I had wanted to sing a male role, I think they would have given it to me! But you have to be very careful with the voice and not change registers indiscriminately. Sometimes, particularly in Italy, certain mezzos jump back and forth between soprano and mezzo parts, which of course is very dangerous.

C.S. Do you think that today's divas are too often careless?

G.V. Quite simply, they sing too much. Even at the start of my career, I never chased after an engagement, no matter what sort it was. I was doing some difficult parts then and would sing four or five times a month. For example, an *Aida,* a *Traviata,* a *Pique Dame,* and a few concerts, but no more.

C.S. A concert is, after all, easier than an opera, isn't it?

G.V. No. I don't agree at all. To sing a whole recital, all by yourself, is a great responsibility. You cannot hide behind a colleague; if you spoil a note, you cannot turn your back to the audience and sing toward the scrim!

C.S. Over the course of a career, a singer's voice changes and she must alter her repertoire.

G.V. That situation has never come up for me. But I do change roles, and then it is I who choose another vocal coloring. In the role of Marguerite, I naturally adopted a clearer and more radiant tone, and my voice had to be less dramatic at the beginning than in the final scenes. As for roles that I should have abandoned, I cannot really think of any. I did dream of singing *Medea* and *Norma*, but those operas weren't in the Bolshoi repertoire. That brings to mind the strange history I had concerning *Tosca*. I added the Puccini opera to my repertoire rather late, around 1969. People always wondered why I didn't sing *Tosca*. Why? Because I had no desire to, because I didn't love the music. One day, Pokrovski came to see me and asked, "Be frank with me: will you agree to sing *Tosca*? I want to do *Tosca* if you are willing to sing the title role. But once you've accepted, don't change your mind!" I replied, "Quite honestly, I must admit that *Tosca* doesn't seem to me like a very interesting opera." He looked at me. "You're an idiot!" Yes, he was my mentor and could allow himself to tell me my home truths. "You were put on this earth to sing *Tosca*!"

C.S. Was he right?

G.V. Today I think he was right. I told him, "I don't agree, but if you say so, I'll go along." The production was mounted. And for a while, Tosca was one of my favorite roles.

C.S. And then one day, everything changed. You, the idol of the Bolshoi, were blacklisted. How did that unfortunate business begin? Did they forbid you to sing?

G.V. No, I was still able to sing as much as I wanted. I occupied too important a position for them to take that sort of step. But they refused to acknowledge my presence! My name was no longer mentioned, neither on television, nor the radio, nor the newspapers; I no longer existed, I was singing in a desert. I could scream all I wanted, but there was no more echo.

C.S. Was the public aware of this?

G.V. No. In the Soviet Union people are so used to someone being mistreated, someone being arrested, someone being killed, that they have become rather indifferent. When we decided to leave the country, a few genuinely concerned people at the Bolshoi asked us, "Why are you leaving? You haven't been arrested, you haven't been thrown in prison!" There are people in the Soviet Union who think like that. They don't understand what it means to take offense and become indignant. Even those who have endured insult and injury don't always understand it.

C.S. I suppose they started by forbidding you to sing abroad?

G.V. You see, and I just told you "I was singing as much as I wanted"—I actually said that! That's how normal it's become in Russia for artists to be prevented from traveling!

C.S. Ten years later you made another decision, but this time you made it yourself, independent of outside pressures. You decided to stop singing on the opera stage. Now that you've taken that step, do you have any regrets?

G.V. No, I'm happy. It's really a relief, and I don't feel the slightest pang. In any case, nothing is changed in my life; I continue to work, I'm singing what I want and will sing as long as my strength permits me. I'm perfectly content. It's strange, but I didn't think I could be so happy to leave the world of opera.

I have one explanation perhaps: I have finally rid myself of that feeling of extreme tension I had every time I went onstage, knowing I wasn't alone, that I depended on others and that my colleagues were counting on me, whether or not there was an understudy— Today, when I give a recital, I rely only on myself, I'm free. In the opera house, even if you're at death's door, you have to go on, you have to provide your series of eight performances. To find an understudy for a Russian opera over here is not very easy!

C.S. This change then is above all another sort of liberation for you—

G.V. Absolutely. This liberty is essential. By nature, I've always been very independent. Even when I was at the Bolshoi and was part of that enormous company, I was still basically a loner. I would go to rehearsal, sing in the performance, and go straight home.

C.S. The opposite of Slava—

G.V. Yes, he has a different nature. He needs to socialize and get together with colleagues. He likes to be part of a group, and that's one of the reasons he insists on working with the National Symphony in Washington.

All this balances our lives. If I had a husband who was as independent as I, I wonder how our lives might have turned out. Or if Slava had married a woman as sociable as he, I'm sure they both would have gone crazy!

C.S. Do you ever try to get him to change?

G.V. It's totally useless. When I met him, I had a lot of trouble accepting his lifestyle. His sociability and the new acquaintances he was always making exasperated me; I couldn't stand it and tried to get him to stop. Later I understood that his whirlwind existence was necessary for him. When he's by himself, he's lost. Sometimes when he returns home, he

204

declares, "My God, what a treat for just the two of us to be alone together! Why don't we live like this all the time?" Yes, that's what he says. So he thinks. But for how long?

So, I've decided not to meddle with his lifestyle. It's just as useless for him to try to change me! From time to time, there's even a storm— Slava functions like a battery that runs down and needs to be recharged all the time. But he does the recharging himself. I know he tires himself out tremendously. Sometimes I feel sorry for him. I worry when I see him working so much and yet know that nothing can be done about it. He comes home after a rehearsal and collapses on his bed. Two hours later, he gets up and goes back out!

C.S. The battery is going to catch his breath: Slava has decided to take a year's sabbatical.

G.V. That's right, and ever since he told us the news, the whole family has been dreading the thought of it. What will he ever be able to do to relax? Will he take apart our whole apartment piece by piece and put it back together again, or chop down all the trees on our American property? We're anxiously wondering and trying to brace ourselves. A year of Slava not working is absolutely unimaginable. We'll be living in an insane asylum!

C.S. Won't the sabbatical year be a chance for Slava and you to take stock after the upheavals of this painful period? What is it like to live in dissidence?

G.V. We are neither dissidents nor defectors! I am simply fighting to uphold a conviction, and I oppose the kind of treatment we had to endure.

I did not "defect." Defectors decide to leave their country and know they will never return. I never made that decision. When we left with the permission to go on a two-year tour, I figured it would last maybe five years but that something would change, that all the trouble would be forgotten and we'd go back home. Today we are stripped of our Soviet citizenship and the page has turned. As long as that regime exists, we will not return to Russia. And that day will not occur in my lifetime. When people as powerful as the directors of the Soviet Communist Party are in power, when they have been able to cast an entire nation into slavery, when they know so well how to manipulate all the advantages and privileges of their situation, I'm convinced that they won't willingly let go of anything or sacrifice an ounce of their power. As for a softening of the Soviet regime's policies, there's always hope, but I know that the regime won't budge an inch, unless there's a war—and if there is a war, we'll all be blown sky-high!

C.S. And yet your life goes on, in Paris, in London, in New York—

G.V. Yes, life goes on. And I have no feeling of emptiness or despair. Who are those contemptible beings who have granted themselves the right to forbid me to live on my native soil? So they took away my citizenship? Do they think I'm a serf that can be thrown into the slave market? I don't even acknowledge their existence! Even if my passport hadn't been taken away, I wouldn't want to live under that regime, for today, for the first time in my life, I'm leading a normal existence, I'm no longer a puppet. As for my Russian blood, who can take that away from me?

C.S. In the morning when you wake up, doesn't your first thought, with equal parts of nostalgia and anger, turn toward Russia?

G.V. I myself never think of it. But Slava often dreams of Moscow. Whenever we happen to be sleeping in separate

206

rooms, I sometimes hear him come and slip into my bed with his pillow under his arm. I can always tell what's wrong! I ask him, "You were in Moscow again?" "Yes, I was," he answers. Frightened, he comes to me for comfort!

Selected Discography

All items included here are in compact-disc format.

The Husband and Wife Team

Britten. *The Poet's Echo.*
> Galina Vishnevskaya, soprano; Mstislav Rostropovich, piano. London 433 200-2.

Mélodies and Romances (by Glinka, Dargomizhsky, Mussorgsky, Borodin, Tchaikovsky).
> Vishnevskaya accompanied by Rostropovich at the piano. Erato 45643-2 (2 discs).

Mussorgsky. *Boris Godunov.*
> Vishnevskaya, Ruggero Raimondi, Paul Plishka, Nicolai Gedda, Vyacheslav Polozov, Catherine Dubosc, National Symphony Orchestra, Oratorio and Choral Arts Societies of Washington, conducted by Rostropovich. Erato 45418-2 (3 discs).

Prokofiev. *War and Peace.*
> Vishnevskaya, Nicolai Gedda, Wieslaw Ochman, Stefania Toczyska, Lajos Miller, Mariana Paunova, Katherine Ciesinski, Dimiter Petkov, Anton Diakov, Malcolm Smith, Nicola Ghiuselev, Michel Sénéchal, Orchestre National de France, Choeurs de Radio France, conducted by Rostropovich. Erato 75480 (4 discs).

Rimsky-Korsakov. "The Heavenly Clouds Disperse."
> Vishnevskaya accompanied by Rostropovich at the piano (live concert in aid of the victims of the Armenian earthquake). RCA Victor Red Seal 7779-2-RC.

Shostakovich. *Lady Macbeth of Mtsensk.*
> Vishnevskaya, Nicolai Gedda, Dimiter Petkov, Werner Krenn, Birgit Finnilä, Robert Tear, London Philharmonic Orchestra, Ambrosian Opera Chorus, conducted by Rostropovich. Angel EMI CDCB 49955 (2 discs).

Shostakovich. Symphony No. 14.

> Vishnevskaya, Mark Reshetin, Moscow Philharmonic Soloists' Ensemble, conducted by Rostropovich. Melodiya SUCD 10-00241.

Tchaikovsky. *Eugene Onegin.*

> Vishnevskaya, Tamara Sinyavskaya, Tatiana Tugarinova, Larissa Avdeyeva, Yuri Mazurok, Vladimir Atlantov, Alexander Ognivtsev, Vitali Vlassov, Bolshoi Theater Orchestra and Chorus, conducted by Rostropovich. Le Chant du Monde LDC 278 485/6 (2 discs).

Tchaikovsky. *Iolanta.*

> Vishnevskaya, Nicolai Gedda, Walton Grönroos, Dimiter Petkov, Tom Krause, Orchestre de Paris, conducted by Rostropovich. Erato 88147 (2 discs).

Galina in Opera

Arias (by Puccini, Verdi, Tchaikovsky).

> Various conductors and orchestras. Melodiya SUCD 10-00654.

Mussorgsky. *Boris Godunov.*

> Nicolai Ghiaurov, Martti Talvela, Ludovico Spiess, Aleksei Maslennikov, Vienna Philharmonic Orchestra, conducted by Herbert von Karajan. London 411 862-2 (3 discs).

Tchaikovsky. *Eugene Onegin.*

> Larissa Avdeyeva, Valentina Petrova, Evgenya Verbitskaya, Sergei Lemeshev, Evgeny Belov, Ivan Petrov, Bolshoi Theater Orchestra and Chorus, conducted by Boris Khaikin. Legato LCD 163-2 (2 discs).

Galina in Concert and Recital

Britten. *War Requiem.*

> Peter Pears, Dietrich Fischer-Dieskau, Melos Ensemble, London Symphony Orchestra, conducted by Benjamin Britten. London 414 383-2 (2 discs).

Mussorgsky. *Bez solnsta* [Sunless], Song Cycle.

> U.S.S.R. Symphony Orchestra, conducted by Evgeny Svetlanov. Melodiya SUCD 10-00178.

Shostakovich. Symphony No. 14.

> Moscow Chamber Orchestra, conducted by Rudolf Barshai. Russian Disc RD CD 11 192.

Rostropovich the Cellist—Chamber Music

Bach, J. C. Trio.
> Jean-Pierre Rampal, flute; Isaac Stern, violin. Sony Classical SK 44568.

Bach, J. S. *Adagio*; Three Chorale Preludes.
> Herbert Tachezi, keyboard. Teldec 77308-2.

Bach, J. S. Unaccompanied Suites No. 2 in D minor and No. 5 in C minor; "Air on the G String"; "Adagio" from *Toccata, Adagio, and Fugue*.
> Vladimir Yampolsky, piano (in "Air" and "Adagio"). Vanguard Classics OVC 4083.

Beethoven. The Complete String Trios.
> Anne-Sophie Mutter, violin; Bruno Giuranna, viola. Deutsche Grammophon 427 687-2 (2 discs).

Beethoven. Five Sonatas for Cello and Piano.
> Sviatoslav Richter, piano. Philips 412 256-2 (2 discs).

Beethoven. Trio No. 6 in B-flat major ("Archduke").
> Emil Gilels, piano; Leonid Kogan, violin. Melodiya SUCD 10-00550.

Brahms. Sonatas in E minor Op. 38, and F major Op. 99.
> Sviatoslav Richter, piano (Op. 38 only). Intaglio 705-1.
> Rudolf Serkin, piano. Deutsche Grammophon 410 510-2.

Britten. Sonata in C major Op. 65; Unaccompanied Suites in G major Op. 72, and D major Op. 80.
> Benjamin Britten, piano (in the Sonata). London 421 859-2.

Caix d'Hervelois, Louis de. *Sieben altfranzösische Mädchenbilder*.
> Herbert Tachezi, keyboard. Teldec 77308-2.

Chopin. Sonata in G minor Op. 65 and *Polonaise brillante* Op. 3.
> Martha Argerich, piano. Deutsche Grammophon 419 860-2.

Debussy. Sonata No. 1 in D minor.
> Benjamin Britten, piano. London 417 833-2.

Fauré. Piano Quartet No. 1, Op. 15.
> Emil Gilels, piano; Leonid Kogan, violin; R. Barchai, viola. Melodiya SUCD 10-00546.

Frescobaldi. *Toccata*.
> Herbert Tachezi, keyboard. Teldec 77308-2.

Handel. "Aria."
> Herbert Tachezi, keyboard. Teldec 77308-2.

Haydn. "London" Trios Nos. 1–4; Divertimentos Op. 100, Nos. 2 and 6.
> Jean-Pierre Rampal, flute; Isaac Stern, violin. CBS MK 37786.

Haydn. Trio No. 19 in G minor.
Emil Gilels, piano; Leonid Kogan, violin. Melodiya SUCD 10-00547.
Marcello. *Adagio.*
Herbert Tachezi, keyboard. Teldec 77308-2.
Mozart. The Complete Flute Quartets.
Jean-Pierre Rampal, flute; Isaac Stern, violin; Bruno Accardo, viola. Sony Classical SK 42320.
Mozart. Piano Trio in G major K. 564.
Emil Gilels, piano; Leonid Kogan, violin. Melodiya SUCD 10-00547.
Mozart. 3 Trios (arr. Divertimenti K. 439b).
Jean-Pierre Rampal, flute; Isaac Stern, violin. Sony Classical SK 44568.
Prokofiev. Sonata in C major Op. 119.
Sviatoslav Richter, piano. Melodiya SUCD 10-00553.
Rachmaninov. Piano Trio No. 2 in D minor.
Pavel Serebryakov, piano; Mikhail Vaiman, violin. Melodiya MEL 10-00504.
Reicha. Variations and Fantasia for Flute, Violin, and Cello Op. 18.
Jean-Pierre Rampal, flute; Isaac Stern, violin. Sony Classical SK 44568.
Rheinberger. Three pieces from Opus 150.
Herbert Tachezi, keyboard. Teldec 77308-2.
Saint-Saëns. *Prière* Op. 158.
Herbert Tachezi, keyboard. Teldec 77308-2.
Saint-Saëns. Trio No. 1 in F major Op. 18.
Emil Gilels, piano; Leonid Kogan, violin. Melodiya SUCD 10-00546.
Schnittke. Piano Trio.
Irina Schnittke, Mark Lubotsky. Sony Classical SK 53271.
Schubert. Sonata for Arpeggione and Piano D. 821.
Benjamin Britten, piano. London 417 833-2.
Schubert. String Quintet in C major D. 956.
Emerson String Quartet. Deutsche Grammophon 431 792-2.
Schubert. String Quintet in C major D. 956.
Melos Quartet. Deutsche Grammophon 415 373-2.
Schumann. *Adagio und Allegro* in A-flat major, Op. 70.
Martha Argerich, piano. Deutsche Grammophon 419 860-2.
Schumann. *Fünf Stücke im Volkston.*
Benjamin Britten, piano. London 417 833-2.
Shostakovich. Piano Trio in E minor Op. 67.

Pavel Serebryakov, piano; Mikhail Vaiman, violin. Melodiya
MEL 10-00504.

Shostakovich. Sonata in D minor Op. 40.
Dmitri Shostakovich, piano. Melodiya SUCD 10-00553.

Tchaikovsky. *Souvenir de Florence.*
Borodin Quartet, Genrikh Talalyan, viola. Melodiya SUCD
10-00238.

Telemann. Quartet for Flute, Violin, Cello, and Lute.
Jean-Pierre Rampal, flute; Isaac Stern, violin; Matthias
Spaeter, lute. Sony Classical SK 44568.

Rostropovich the Cellist—with Orchestra

Babadjanyan. Concerto.
Moscow Philharmonic Orchestra, conducted by Kirill Kondrashin. Russian Disc RD CD 11 115.

Bach, C. P. E. Concerto No. 2 in B-flat major Wq 171.
Moscow Chamber Orchestra, conducted by Rudolf Barshai
(live). Russian Disc RD CD 11 113.
Saint Paul Chamber Orchestra, conducted by Hugh Wolff.
Teldec 77311-2.

Beethoven. Triple Concerto in C major Op. 56.
Sviatoslav Richter, piano; David Oistrakh, violin. Berlin Phil-
harmonic, conducted by Herbert von Karajan. EMI
CDM 64744.

Bloch. *Schelomo.*
Orchestre National de France, conducted by Leonard Bern-
stein. EMI CDC 49307.
U.S.S.R. Radio and Television Orchestra, conducted by Yuri
Ahronovich. Russian Disc RD CD 11 002.

Boccherini. Concerto in D major.
Zürich Collegium Musicum, conducted by Paul Sacher.
Deutsche Grammophon 429 098.

Brahms. Double Concerto in A minor.
Boris Gutnikov, violin; U.S.S.R. Symphony Orchestra, con-
ducted by Boris Khaikin. Russian Disc RD CD 11 114.
David Oistrakh, violin; Cleveland Orchestra, conducted by
George Szell. EMI CDM 64744.
Itzhak Perlman, violin; London Symphony Orchestra, con-
ducted by Gennadi Rozhdestvensky. Intaglio 7131.

Britten. Symphony for Cello and Orchestra Op. 68.
English Chamber Orchestra, conducted by Benjamin Britten.

London 425 100-2.

    Moscow Philharmonic Orchestra, conducted by Benjamin Britten. Russian Disc RD CD 11 108.

Casadesus, H. G. Concerto in C minor (formerly attributed to J. C. Bach).

    Moscow Chamber Orchestra, conducted by Rudolf Barshai (live). Russian Disc RD CD 11 113.

Dutilleux. Concerto.

    Orchestre de Paris, conducted by Serge Baudo. EMI Classics CDC 7 49304 2.

Dvořák. Concerto in B minor Op. 104.

    Berlin Philharmonic, conducted by Herbert von Karajan. Deutsche Grammophon 413 819-2.

    Boston Symphony Orchestra, conducted by Seiji Ozawa. Erato 45252-2.

    Czech Philharmonic, conducted by V. Talich. Supraphon 111327-2.

    London Philharmonic Orchestra, conducted by Carlo Maria Giulini. EMI CDC 49306.

    U.S.S.R. Symphony Orchestra, conducted by Boris Khaikin. Russian Disc RD CD 11 114.

    U.S.S.R. Television and Radio Large Symphony Orchestra, conducted by Boris Khaikin. Melodiya SUCD 10-00548.

Elgar. Concerto in E minor Op. 85.

    London Symphony Orchestra, conducted by Gennadi Rozhdestvensky. Intaglio INCD 7301.

Glazunov. *Chant du ménestrel.*

    Boston Symphony Orchestra, conducted by Seiji Ozawa. Deutsche Grammophon 431 475-2.

Haydn. Concertos in C major and D major.

    Academy of St.-Martin-in-the-Fields, conducted by Iona Brown. EMI CDC 49305.

    U.S.S.R. Radio and Television Orchestra, conducted by Yuri Ahronovich (D major only). Russian Disc RD CD 11 002.

Hindemith. Concerto.

    U.S.S.R. Radio and Television Orchestra, conducted by Yuri Ahronovich. Russian Disc RD CD 11 002.

Hoddinott. *Noctis Equi.*

    London Symphony Orchestra, conducted by Kent Nagano. Erato 45489-2.

Honegger. Concerto.

> London Symphony Orchestra, conducted by Kent Nagano. Erato 45489-2.

> London Symphony Orchestra, conducted by Gennadi Rozhdestvensky. Intaglio ING 7391.

> U.S.S.R. Symphony Orchestra, conducted by Victor Dubrovsky. Russian Disc RD CD 11 101.

Khachaturian. Concerto-Rhapsody.

> U.S.S.R. Radio and Television Large Symphony Orchestra, conducted by Aram Khachaturian (live 1973 concert). Russian Disc RD CD 11 014.

Khrennikov. Concerto Op. 16.

> U.S.S.R. Radio and Television Large Symphony Orchestra, conducted by Gennadi Rozhdestvensky. Russian Disc RD CD 11 110.

Knipper. *Concerto-monologue* in C major.

> Moscow Philharmonic Orchestra, conducted by Gennadi Rozhdestvensky. Russian Disc RD CD 11 111.

Lalo. Concerto in D minor.

> U.S.S.R. Symphony Orchestra, conducted by Victor Dubrovsky. Russian Disc RD CD 11 101.

Levitin. Concertino in E minor Op. 54.

> U.S.S.R. Symphony Orchestra, conducted by Kirill Kondrashin. Russian Disc RD CD 11 111.

Lutoslawski. *Tout un monde lointain.*

> Orchestre de Paris, conducted by W. Lutoslawski. EMI Classics CDC 7 49304 2.

Matthews, David. *Romanza* for Cello and Small Orchestra, Op. 49.

> English Chamber Orchestra, conducted by Raymond Leppard (live performance at Buckingham Palace, August 1990). EMI CDC 54164.

Messiaen. *La Transfiguration de Notre Seigneur Jésus-Christ.*

> National Symphony Orchestra, Westminster Symphonic Choir, conducted by Antal Dorati. London 425616-2.

Milhaud. Concerto No. 1.

> London Symphony Orchestra, conducted by Kent Nagano. Erato 45489-2.

Moret. Concerto.

> Zürich Collegium Musicum, conducted by Paul Sacher. Erato 45530-2.

Panufik. Concerto.
London Symphony Orchestra, conducted by Hugh Wolff. NMC CD 010S.

Prokofiev (completed by M. Rostropovich, orchestrated by Kabalevsky). *Concertino* in G minor.
London Symphony Orchestra, conducted by Gennadi Rozhdestvensky. Intaglio INCD 7301.

Prokofiev. *Sinfonia Concertante* Op. 125.
Leningrad Philharmonic Symphony Orchestra, conducted by Kurt Sanderling. Melodiya SUCD 10-00549.
London Symphony Orchestra, conducted by Seiji Ozawa. Erato 45332-2.

Saint-Saëns. Concerto No. 1.
London Philharmonic Orchestra, conducted by Carlo Maria Giulini. EMI CDC 49306.
U.S.S.R. Symphony Orchestra, conducted by Victor Dubrovsky. Russian Disc RD CD 11 101.
U.S.S.R. Television and Radio Symphony Orchestra, conducted by G. Stolyarov. Melodiya SUCD 10-00549.

Sauget. *Mélodie concertante.*
U.S.S.R. Symphony Orchestra, conducted by Henri Sauget. Russian Disc RD CD 11 108.

Schnittke. Concerto No. 2.
London Symphony Orchestra, conducted by Seiji Ozawa. Sony Classical SK 48241.

Schumann. Concerto in A minor Op. 129.
Moscow Philharmonic, conducted by David Oistrakh. Russian Disc RD CD 11 106.
Moscow Philharmonic, conducted by Samuil Samosud. Melodiya SUCD 10-00548.
Orchestre National de France, conducted by Leonard Bernstein. EMI CDC 49307.

Shostakovich. Concerto No. 1.
Czech Philharmonic, conducted by Kirill Kondrashin. Intaglio 7251.
London Symphony Orchestra, conducted by Seiji Ozawa. Erato 45332-2.
Philadelphia Orchestra, conducted by Eugene Ormandy. CBS Masterworks Portrait MPK 44850.
U.S.S.R. Symphony Orchestra, conducted by David Oistrakh. Russian Disc RD CD 11 106.
U.S.S.R. Symphony Orchestra, conducted by Evgeny

Svetlanov. Russian Disc RD CD 11 109.

Shostakovich. Concerto No. 2.

Boston Symphony Orchestra, conducted by Seiji Ozawa. Deutsche Grammophon 431 475-2.

London Symphony Orchestra, conducted by Gennadi Rozhdestvensky. Intaglio 7251.

U.S.S.R. Symphony Orchestra, conducted by Evgeny Svetlanov. Russian Disc RD CD 11 109.

Strauss, R. *Don Quixote.*

London Symphony Orchestra, conducted by Gennadi Rozhdestvensky. Intaglio ING 7391.

Tartini. Concerto in A major.

Moscow Chamber Orchestra, conducted by Rudolf Barshai (live). Russian Disc RD CD 11 113.

Tartini. Concerto in D major.

Saint Paul Chamber Orchestra, conducted by Hugh Wolff. Teldec 77311-2.

Zürich Collegium Musicum, conducted by Paul Sacher. Deutsche Grammophon 429 098.

Tchaikovsky, Boris. Concerto.

Moscow Philharmonic Orchestra, conducted by Kirill Kondrashin. Russian Disc RD CD 11 115.

Tchaikovsky, P. I. *Andante cantabile.*

Boston Symphony Orchestra, conducted by Seiji Ozawa. Deutsche Grammophon 431 475-2.

Tchaikovsky, P. I. *Pezzo capriccioso* Op. 62.

London Symphony Orchestra, conducted by Gennadi Rozhdestvensky. Intaglio INCD 7301.

U.S.S.R. Radio and Television Large Symphony Orchestra, conducted by Gennadi Rozhdestvensky. Russian Disc RD CD 11 110.

Tchaikovsky, P. I. *Variations on a Rococo Theme* Op. 33.

Berlin Philharmonic Orchestra, conducted by Herbert von Karajan. Deutsche Grammophon 431 606-2 or 413 819-2.

Boston Symphony Orchestra, conducted by Seiji Ozawa. Erato 45252-2.

Leningrad Philharmonic Orchestra, conducted by Gennadi Rozhdestvensky. Melodiya SUCD 10-00238.

London Symphony Orchestra, conducted by Gennadi Rozhdestvensky. Intaglio INCD 7081.

Vainberg. Concerto in C minor Op. 43.
> Moscow Philharmonic Orchestra, conducted by Gennadi Rozhdestvensky. Russian Disc RD CD 11 111.

Vivaldi. Concertos RV 413 and RV 417.
> Moscow Chamber Orchestra, conducted by Rudolf Barshai (live). Russian Disc RUS CD 11 113.

Vivaldi. Concerto in D minor RV 406.
> Saint Paul Chamber Orchestra, conducted by Hugh Wolff. Teldec 77311-2.

Vivaldi. Concertos in C major P. 31, and G major P. 120.
> Zürich Collegium Musicum, conducted by Paul Sacher. Deutsche Grammophon 429 098.

Vlasov. Concerto.
> U.S.S.R. Radio and Television Large Symphony Orchestra, conducted by Gennadi Rozhdestvensky. Russian Disc RD CD 11 110.

Rostropovich the Conductor

Chopin. Piano Concerto No. 2 in F minor.
> Martha Argerich, piano. National Symphony Orchestra. Deutsche Grammophon 419 859-2.

Prokofiev. *Alexander Nevsky* and *Ivan the Terrible.*
> Dolora Zajick (*Alexander Nevsky*) and Christopher Plummer, Tamara Sinyavskaya, Sergei Leiferkus, New London Children's Choir (*Ivan the Terrible*). London Symphony Orchestra and Chorus. Sony Classical S2K 48387 (2 discs).

Prokofiev. *Romeo and Juliet,* Suites Nos. 1 and 2.
> National Symphony Orchestra. Deutsche Grammophon 410 519-2.

Prokofiev. Symphonies Nos. 1–7.
> Orchestre National de France. Erato 45707-2 (4 discs).

Prokofiev. Violin Concerto No. 2.
> Anne-Sophie Mutter, violin; National Symphony Orchestra. Erato 45708-2.

Rachmaninov. *Vespers,* Op. 37.
> Maureen Forrester, Gene Tucker, Choral Arts Society of Washington. Erato 45269-2.

Return to Russia.
> Live concert at the Moscow Conservatory in February 1990, marking the return of Mstislav Rostropovich to his

homeland after an absence of sixteen years; he conducts the National Symphony Orchestra in Tchaikovsky's Symphony No. 6 and in encores by Johann Strauss/arr. Shostakovich, Grieg, Paganini, Prokofiev, Gershwin, Sousa. Sony Classical SK 45836.

Schnittke. *In memoriam.* . . .
    London Symphony Orchestra. Sony Classical SK 48241.

Schnittke. *Life with an Idiot.*
    Teresa Ringholz, Dale Duesing/Romain Bischoff, Howard Haskin, Robin Leggate, Netherlands Opera, Rotterdam Philharmonic. Sony Classical S2K 52495 (2 discs).

Schnittke. Viola Concerto.
    Yuri Bashmet, viola; London Symphony Orchestra. RCA Victor Red Seal 60446-2-RC.

Shostakovich. *Rauok* [Learner's Manual].
    Nicolai Ghiuselev, Nikita Storojev, Romuald Tesarowicz, Arcadi Volodos (Russian version); Jonathan Deutsch, Eric Halfvrason, Julian Rodescu, Andrew Wentzel (English version), conducted at the piano by Rostropovich. Erato 75571.

Shostakovich. Symphony No. 5.
    National Symphony Orchestra. Deutsche Grammophon 410 509-2.

Shostakovich. Symphony No. 7 ("Leningrad").
    National Symphony Orchestra. Erato 45414-2.

Shostakovich. Symphony No. 8.
    National Symphony Orchestra. Teldec 74719-2.

Shostakovich. Symphony No. 10.
    London Symphony Orchestra. Teldec 74529-2.

Shostakovich. Symphony No. 11 ("The Year 1905").
    National Symphony Orchestra. Teldec 76262-2.

Shostakovich. Symphony No. 13 ("Babi Yar").
    Nicola Ghiuselev, bass; National Symphony Orchestra, Men of the Choral Arts Society of Washington. Erato 45349-2.

Shostakovich. Symphony No. 15.
    London Symphony Orchestra. Teldec 74560-2.

Tchaikovsky. *Capriccio italien.*
    Berlin Philharmonic Orchestra. Deutsche Grammophon 431 610-2.

Tchaikovsky. Piano Concertos Nos. 1 and 3.
    Vladimir Feltsman, piano. National Symphony Orchestra. Sony Classical SK 45756.

Tchaikovsky. Suites from *Swan Lake, The Sleeping Beauty,* and *The Nutcracker.*
   Berlin Philharmonic Orchestra. Deutsche Grammophon 429 097-2.
Tchaikovsky. Symphony No. 5 and *1812 Overture.*
   National Symphony Orchestra. Erato 45415-2.
Tchaikovsky. Symphony No. 6 ("Pathétique").
   See *Return to Russia.*
Villa-Lobos. *Bachianas Brasileiras* No. 1.
   Cellos of the English Chamber Orchestra (live concert in aid of the victims of the Armenian earthquake). RCA Victor Red Seal 7779-2-RC.

On Video

Soldiers of Music: Rostropovich Returns to Russia.
   A film by Susan Froemke, Peter Gelb, Albert Maysles, Bob Eisenhardt. With Mike Wallace, Mstislav Rostropovich, Galina Vishnevskaya, Olga Rostropovich, National Symphony Orchestra. Music by Barber, Dvořák, Grieg, Puccini, Prokofiev, Rachmaninoff, Shostakovich, Tchaikovsky. Sony Classical 46387 (VHS or laser disc).

Index of Names